SINGLE-
MINDED

SINGLE-MINDED

My Life in Business

CLAUDE LITTNER

piatkus

PIATKUS

First published in Great Britain in 2016 by Piatkus

Copyright © Claude Littner 2016

1 3 5 7 9 10 8 6 4 2

A CIP catalogue record for this book
is available from the British Library.

Hardback ISBN 978-0-349-41452-2
Trade paperback ISBN 978-0-349-41451-5

London EC4Y 0DZ

An Hachette UK Company
www.hachette.co.uk

www.improvementzone.co.uk

To Max, Freddie and Sienna who have
their whole lives ahead of them

In memory of Harrison and Jemima
who were not given the gift of life

Contents

Contents

Foreword

I met Claude some 25 years ago, and threw him in at the deep end to 'steady the ship' in Amstrad's French subsidiary. It was never going to be an easy fix, but Claude managed the whole process in a thorough and professional manner. He fulfilled the same function in Spain, and I was in no doubt that I had found a very capable and forthright individual, who could be relied on to give me his honest opinion based on the facts.

As Chief Executive of Spurs, Claude did not shy away from making unpopular decisions, but they were absolutely in line with best business practice, and he was able to put in place many of the business processes and structures that were lacking. In doing so, he occasionally fell out with the playing staff and media, but this was all within his remit of resolving the issues at hand and the guidelines I had set out.

Over the years, he has continued to prove himself in business both within my group of companies and independently, and has been highly successful in turning around a number of very poorly performing companies. I give him great credit for that, and it further demonstrates his business acumen and strength of character.

Claude has been with me since the start of *The Apprentice,* making the interview episode his own by expertly scrutinising each year's final candidates' CVs and business plans, and occasionally finding them seriously flawed. This has been most helpful to me in determining which candidate will become the eventual winner and, most recently, my business partner. Claude was therefore a natural choice when Nick Hewer relinquished his position, as I know that nothing much escapes his critical eye.

Having read *Single-Minded*, I have found it to be a very enjoyable read. It is very honest and engaging, much like the man himself, and should be recommended reading for anyone who aspires to make their way in business, either as an employee or a would-be entrepreneur. It is instructive and entertaining, providing an interesting insight into the ups and downs of business life and showing how single-mindedness, openness and determination can yield dividends both financial and personal.

Alan Sugar
London
July 2016

'Sugar, but no milk!'

You know the way some days just stick in your mind? My first day at Tottenham Hotspur was one of those days.

It was the beginning of November 1993, and I was about to take up my position as chief executive of Tottenham Hotspur – the team I had supported all my life. The club was haemorrhaging money and Alan Sugar had drafted me in to sort it out. Everywhere you looked, there was a problem.

I walked up to the main stadium entrance at White Hart Lane in North London, and there, almost entirely blocking the way, were a number of crates containing bottles of milk. I neatly sidestepped them and made my way to my office and a very busy day ahead. I worked until late in the evening and, as I left the stadium, I reflected on the challenges that lay ahead and the thrill of really getting stuck in. I noticed that the crates of milk, untouched since the morning, were still blocking the entrance, but thought nothing further of it.

The next day the bottles of milk were still there and, stacked alongside them, was a second load. This time I asked Audrey, the PA to club secretary Peter Barnes, about the milk. 'Ah, that's very simple, Mr Littner. Sometimes the manager trains the team here, so we always arrange to have milk ready for the players. The team mostly trains at the Mill Hill training ground, but as we never know what the plans are, we always have a daily order of milk, just in case.'

This is just silly, I thought. 'Right, Audrey, this is what we are going to do. Tell the milkman: no more milk to be delivered here. And if Mr Ardiles [then manager] turns up to train here, someone can head off to Tesco and buy milk.'

Sure enough, the next day no milk appeared. The milkman was very upset indeed, since we were his biggest account, but he was by no means the only person I unwittingly upset over the coming years. The following Saturday, Spurs lost and the newspapers got hold of the milk story. 'Sugar But No Milk!' screamed one huge headline, linking the cancellation of the milk with the team's poor performance. Welcome to the world of Premier League football, I thought.

Cancelling the milk didn't make a jot of difference to the club's accounts (nor to its performance on the pitch), but it is characteristic of the way I work. If I see examples of silliness, I stop it. That may really upset people, but I am focused on the task in hand: cutting costs where appropriate and making sure that overheads are scrutinised. Nothing escapes my attention.

Even after the milk incident, I felt sure I could cope with anything that the football club, the media, the fans and the playing staff could throw at me. I'm pretty tough and resilient. People watch me on *The Apprentice* and see someone who frightens the living daylights out of hopeful candidates – aggressively, forensically dismantling their business plans, or their often less-than-hundred-per-cent-truthful CVs. They see me dismissing candidates from the interviews, crushing their hopes and egos in the process. 'Tough', 'unforgiving', 'exacting' are some of the printable words that have been bandied about with regard to my business style. And I am, or have been, all of those things in my business life, driven by an unwavering desire to do everything thoroughly, and always to the very best of my ability.

I work relentlessly until a job is done and the company in question has been turned around and is able to stand on its own two feet. The one thing I am not, though, is ruthless. I want to get things done efficiently and honestly – and I take pains to show people what that means and how to do it. I give them a fair chance, but if they mess me about, or if they can't or won't fall in line and accept the new order, then I move them on without further ado. However, I don't like doing it and, to be fair, most people 'get it', feel liberated, knuckle down to hard work and reap the rewards.

What viewers see in *The Apprentice* is what some of my former colleagues might well have been subjected to in other boardrooms. I am, as the title of this book suggests, single-minded. But I am single-minded about wanting the best for the company I'm working for, not in my desire to upset or cause people distress.

*

My upbringing might have indicated that I would become a very different kind of personality to the one I am today.

My parents provided the most stable, loving and secure environment anyone could wish for, and I loved them very much. My mother was someone I could go to with a problem at any time; she was always compassionate and involved in my daily life – I called or saw her every day to the very end of her life.

My father had a wonderful personality and was a smart businessman, but of a completely different mindset to me. I certainly benefited from the deep sense of strength and security he provided, but as a child I felt that he was a bit distant or aloof – a quality that, perhaps, isn't uncommon for men of his generation. I also think that I disappointed him. I believe I did so many times, although other family members assure me that he was always very proud of me. But he never told me that himself. And I certainly didn't achieve anything at school to make him proud.

My relationship with my father only really blossomed when I started to take responsibility for myself – when I could talk business with him. When I gained some independence and started to make my own decisions, we talked a lot. And his values, his prudence and his risk-averse position, held for such good reasons, have had a big influence on me and the way that I work. I owe both my parents more than I can express.

My father grew up in a Jewish family in Vienna, Austria during one of the most oppressive and dangerous periods in recent history. He and his brother were dispatched to school in Brighton in 1937 when he was fourteen, although they didn't have a word of English between them. Their parents stayed in Europe: my grandfather was in banking and had property and business interests there.

Then, one summer holiday during the war, my father went to occupied Paris to meet up with his parents. He and my grandfather were caught and interned in the velodrome. They escaped from there – I don't know how because my father never talked about his experiences in the war – and made their way to Portugal. En route, by a miracle, they met up with my grandmother and the three of them obtained documents to show they were Cubans who were being repatriated to their 'homeland'. They subsequently lived in Havana for some years before eventually making it to the USA.

After the war, my father went to university in New York and met my mother, a native New Yorker. I was born in the city in 1949. When I was two years old, just after my sister was born, we moved to London so my father could join his brother and a family friend who had started a carpet wholesale business. The business flourished in the post-war decades, all the way through to the nineties, even helping to create one of the biggest brands in the UK at the time – Allied Carpets.

The three business partners were tenacious and enterprising businessmen. They discussed and argued all the time – that was their creative way of decision-making and conducting business. They all contributed in their own ways, and they were all impeccable gentlemen with the highest ethical standards. So many of that generation ended up becoming solid, reliable people with good values. They had survived the war and somehow that gave them a different view of life.

By the time we moved to London, there was nothing of my grandfather's business or property left in Europe, and he himself had just passed away. My father was only twenty-eight at the time. That loss, and the loss of so many family members during the Holocaust, had had a profound effect on him. He was determined to secure his family's future, to seek out a safe environment, and to enjoy life.

So my parents focused on keeping hold of what they had, and were never over-ambitious. They were savers and that is something they have certainly passed on to me. In Britain after the war, the contrast between the privations and dangers of wartime and the sense of opportunity, freedom and potential of the post-war years was immense. For my parents, being in a relatively affluent situation meant that they could enjoy their lives, as long as they lived within their means.

Family was at the heart of everything. When they arrived in England they had few friends, and so my father, his brother Ken and their business partner, Henry, relied on each other for friendship and entertainment. And of course their business – and business in general – was inevitably a part of the conversation when the families got together for tea on Sunday or on other occasions. Our families saw each other constantly, so the business conversations were part of the soundtrack of my childhood.

My father's approach to industrial relations was completely paternalistic. I remember the company taking on a temporary driver. That 'temporary driver', as he was always known, was with the firm for over thirty years and eventually became the warehouse manager. The employees were all treated as family and looked after by the company; if employees had a problem, the business would give them extra money. And no one ever left the company! In hindsight, it was remarkable. And I learned a lot about the value of loyalty and being fair and honourable from that.

The business grew steadily and received a number of takeover approaches over the years. Each one was rejected, apparently because the price was calculated to be unacceptable, but I think it had more to do with the fact that the business was an integral part of the owners' lives. They enjoyed working and the daily routine of going to the office. What would they do every day instead? Inevitably, they held on too long, didn't move with the times, and the business gradually lost its dynamism.

My father was a good businessman, with lots of charm and charisma, and he was much gentler than I am. He didn't have big ambitions, but he was hard-working, shrewd, entrepreneurial and level-headed. He always made his margin, but he wasn't driven by a desire slavishly to grow the business, or to sell out. He and my uncles ran the business to provide for themselves and their families, and to have fun doing it. When I reflect on their business, I love their ethos, but feel they didn't respond quickly enough to the structural changes in the industry. They also didn't relinquish control when it was time to give my cousins, who had joined the business, the opportunity to take the reins. I think subconsciously that lesson got through to me, and I am now always looking to see how I can help, encourage and bring on young people.

My ambitions, though not my ability, were on a different scale to my father's. I had a deeper, greater need – perhaps because of my schooldays, or even simply because of the way I am – to prove myself. My character is more edgy, if you like – less easily settled.

And I don't do easy. That's my problem.

'Littner, *fond de la classe*'

If there's anything that has driven me to write this book, it's to get the message out to all young people that, even if your school career doesn't turn out the way you or your parents would have liked, if you can find a path that works for you, if you want it and are prepared to work hard enough to achieve it, then there is always opportunity.

A few years after moving to London, my parents befriended a family with a precocious daughter, who went to the Lycée Français de Londres in South Kensington. As my father was a 'European', he thought it would be great for me to learn a foreign language. So, as a confident and excited four-year-old, I went there.

My first day at the Lycée, 1953.

The Lycée was completely French speaking, which means that my entire schooling was conducted in French. It'll become apparent why this was important later on, but, for a long time, I thought being bilingual was pointless. And, taken as a whole, my time at the Lycée was pretty bloody miserable.

Having made a really good start, from around the age of eight, it started to go very wrong. I have no idea why, but from being an excellent student, suddenly my reports and grades plummeted. So much so that at the beginning of each academic year, the new teacher would start by calling out 'Littner' and, when I tentatively raised my hand, the teacher would say '*fond de la classe*' (back of the classroom) where I was to sit in failure and humiliation. I became extremely disruptive and naughty, and my end-of-term reports were a source of great frustration to my father.

Don't get me wrong, the Lycée was, and is, an excellent school, but it just didn't suit me. During my whole school life to the age of seventeen, I struggled.

Looking back on it, I think I just didn't get the French way of teaching at that time. I can't learn things by heart and regurgitate them; I actually have to understand them. Learning a twenty-line poem or a piece of meaningless prose, or recounting the origins of Jansenism (French theology) parrot fashion for the sake of it, just doesn't work for me.

The one subject I always excelled at was maths, but in almost every other subject, the comments from the teachers were 'lazy', 'very lazy', 'talks too much', 'doesn't pay attention', 'could do better' and so on. On one occasion, a comment on my report changed from 'very lazy' to 'lazy', an improvement that didn't carry much weight with my father, despite my cheeky protestations.

There was something at the Lycée called the '*tableau d'honneur*' which was a termly award for good work or improved performance. The headmistress at the time was a Mme Seriax, who was a horrible and vindictive woman always dressed in black. The normal code was to read out only the names of the pupils who had reached the required standard and omit those who had not. However, she used to take particular delight in calling out my name and, during those few split seconds, allow me to experience joy, only to narrow her eyes and say, '*NON!*' It was a crushing disappointment almost every term.

Every Monday morning we'd have a written test on a subject that we were supposed to have memorised over the weekend. As I was '*fond de la classe*', no one cared that I had a genuine problem and simply couldn't do it. So, my best friend Leonard, another '*fond de la classe*' victim, and I did whatever we could to disrupt, postpone or get out of sitting the test. We'd come in early and take all our classmates' pens away so no one had anything to write with, or move the teacher's desk to the front of the platform it stood on, so that it toppled off. On one occasion I flooded the classroom by turning on all the taps in the toilets on the floor above, and another time I set fire to the classroom lino. I was a very disruptive, naughty boy!

My inability to regurgitate pointless information contrasted strongly with my commercial acumen. From an early age, I was buying gobstoppers in bulk for a ha'penny and very successfully selling them on to my school friends for a penny. This was just one of a number of money-making enterprises I was engaged in.

In an effort not to come too near the bottom of the class, I would also resort to cheating. On one occasion we had to learn all about the French mountains. I didn't, and couldn't see the point of that, so I copied all the facts from the book onto a few sheets of paper. On the Monday morning I pretended to sit the test, but actually just handed in the copied answers. I was pretty confident that I'd be top of the class that week. When the teacher came to read out the results though, I remember, the class genius Michael Laing came

Classroom antics.

top with a hundred per cent. Oh well, second, I thought. But I wasn't second – or even third. When the teacher had reached the end of the register and my name still hadn't been called, I realised I might be in a spot of bother. She called me to the front of the class and asked me to recite some key facts about Mont Blanc. Of course, I hadn't a clue, because I hadn't, and couldn't have, learned them. Another deep humiliation.

To compound the problem, I was very bloody-minded. One of the school's favourite minor punishments was to be given lines. As this was a fairly regular occurrence for me, instead of trying to do my homework, I would spend my time preparing lines for punishment yet to be meted out. If the next day I did something untoward, and the teacher would say, '*Littner, cent fois* ... "*Je suis un bavard*"' ('A hundred times ... "I am a chatterbox"') or something like that, I'd reach into my schoolbag and hand over the lines I'd written the night before – even counting out the number of pages according to the number of lines I'd been set. Appalling behaviour. But it felt good!

My parents, to be fair, did try and move me to a different school, but the problem was that the French and English curricula just didn't match. So, I sat Haberdashers, City of London and St Paul's entrance exams, but because the little I had learned was about French history, French geography, the way the French tackled mathematics, I failed all of them.

I remember distinctly one interview, for University College School, in which I was asked to solve a long division problem. I could do it easily, but the French method was so different from the English one that the headmaster couldn't comprehend it, and I didn't get accepted.

Many years later, I happened to run into Kenneth, an older boy who lived at the bottom of my road when we were growing up. I was surprised when he mentioned that we had something in common, apart from living in the same road. Yes, he stated, 'We both went to Haberdashers.' He must have seen me taking the entrance exam there on so many occasions that he thought I was actually a pupil at the school!

At seventeen, mercifully, I left the Lycée, and I remember my careers master, Mr Morgan, saying to me, 'Claude, you will never amount to anything.' It has stuck with me to this day, and is a painful reminder of my school days.

From what I have reflected of my years at the Lycée, you might have come to the conclusion that I didn't care whether I succeeded or not. That is just not the case. I really did want to succeed, but I just didn't know how to study or get meaningless information into my head, only to regurgitate it a few days later. Looking back, I can see how that feeling of failure, and not being good enough, has fuelled a lot of my decisions and attitude. I always want to do the very best I can in whatever task I'm given. It doesn't matter if it's doing a pointless and repetitive study, negotiating a footballer's contract, or running a company – I always want to show myself to the very best of my ability.

*

My academic career was rescued when I decided to take control of my future and go to Barnet College to do an OND (Ordinary National Diploma) in Business Studies and A levels. Finally, I embarked on studying subjects I was interested in: finance, law, economics, *business*. These subjects bore some relation to the world around me, and I was absorbed by them and couldn't get enough! No more physics, chemistry, Latin, Spanish and *French*. My law teacher Mr Barden took a particular interest in me and, lo and behold, I got a 'B' in my Law A level. To me it just shows how important a part of the teacher's role it is to stimulate the interest of their students.

By moving to Barnet College, the terrible academic baggage I had carried around at the Lycée vanished and I found myself among ordinary people who just wanted to get on. And so did I. I even became something of a star – ironically because I could speak fluent French!

Up to the moment that I started at Barnet, school had

been a depressing and stressful series of humiliations and failures. If I'd been interviewing me at the time, I'd probably have just said 'Get out' and not looked up from my desk. Apart from maths, I couldn't learn what the teachers wanted me to, and I didn't understand *why* I was supposed to learn it. Yet when I run companies, or am sitting next to Alan Sugar in *The Apprentice* boardroom with seven million viewers glued to their television screens, sometimes I think back to Mr Morgan's assessment of me and reflect that I have come quite a long way for a naughty boy who couldn't get on at school.

Early encounters with
the greasy corporate pole

Every company I have worked for has provided me with insights into how big organisations work – none more so than the first two roles I held. Work experience is something I'm always trying to cultivate in my role at the Claude Littner Business School by encouraging companies to take interns, so that our students can see what a job is like in reality. Real experience of a workplace is about the most valuable training you can get (apart from technical qualifications, obviously), because seeing how people work and interact in business provides an important head start in understanding what you want to do in life. This was certainly true of my first contact with work.

After Barnet, I decided to enrol on a BA Honours degree in Business Studies at the University of West London. The course involved six months' study alternating with six months in industry over a four-year period. But to secure a place, I needed a company to sponsor me. The college had a list of potential placements and I wrote to a lot of them. Some weren't interested; others invited me in for interview. One of these was Lucas CAV – a well-established car and commercial vehicle component manufacturer. They made fuel injection systems for diesel engines, car batteries, and so on. It was a business that had been doing well, but was now facing competitive pressure from German companies entering the UK market, coupled with the decline of the UK motor manufacturing industry.

A friend from Barnet, Jeffrey Hyman, and I both passed the interview and joined them at their offices in Acton, West London. Apart from the directors' area, the place was spartan, with bare fluorescent lighting, prison-like windows, and a factory floor that was labour intensive and grim. In other ways, it was very quaint. At 11.00 a.m. and 4.00 p.m., the tea lady would come round the offices with a trolley. She'd pour you a cup of tea and give her favourites a slice of cake!

It was 1968. I was nineteen and bright-eyed, looking forward to my first work placement. I arrived and they handed me a massive tome of a 'time and motion' study. The authors, Mead and Carney, had analysed, under laboratory conditions, the time it takes for a person to undertake mundane clerical tasks. For example, how long it takes to blink, turn a page, pick up a pencil, look at a number, draw breath, and so on. I went on a course just to understand the methods described in the book. Mind-numbing . . . and, even in the 1960s, completely out of date!

I was asked to apply my findings to assess a department in the company. This consisted of fifteen clerks sitting in a column, each processing a variety of documents. My job was to monitor in the minutest detail the 'productivity' of each one of these fifteen people, using the Mead–Carney timings for each specific activity. Can you imagine doing that? It took me six months. At the end of all this I had worked out how much time each of them took to perform their tasks.

The purpose of the exercise was plainly to give legitimacy to the premise that the same amount of work could actually be done by fewer people. The result? Three people were laid off. They weren't bad workers or even lazy – they just fell foul of a stupid, outmoded formula and management style, which treated people as machines. It was a horrible, soul-destroying six months of my life, and typified the culture of the company: full of totally backward-looking attitudes.

For example, on my first day I visited Mrs Isherwood (a director's wife) who sat in a 'cage' with all the stationery supplies. She allocated me a pencil and a pad of paper, both of which I needed to sign for. Within a few days I had lost my pencil. I didn't think anything of it, but when I went to ask for a replacement, I was refused. You were only allowed to get a new pencil when the one you had been issued with was down to a stub. It was a cartoon version of a Victorian business.

Meanwhile, others were taking advantage of the company and getting away with petty theft and pilfering. One of my six-month stints was in the marketing department, where staff would requisition a car battery for 'photographic purposes'. They would take some photos and the battery would then disappear into one of the blokes' Ford Cortina! The staff didn't really need it for their marketing; they just needed a new battery. So, on the one hand you had a company that wouldn't issue more than one pencil at a time, while, simultaneously, some staff were nicking costly items. Absolutely diabolical!

While the whole exercise was a low point, it was also very instructive. From observing how my father's company was run, I had seen how management and staff could collaborate in a business and, by contrast, I had now seen how they could be at loggerheads at Lucas CAV. When, later in my career, I came to be in a senior position, I was acutely aware of the sort of management style I wanted to adopt. To me, it made no sense to create a divide between the two, so I have always been careful to be as visible and accessible to the workforce as possible. Whether they like it is another matter, of course!

I also learned a lot about how management should and shouldn't behave, and how their words and actions affect staff. Respect is key in this: realise that everyone contributes – or should contribute – and respect and try to understand the work that they do. It's essential to make sure that the board-room, management and the 'shop floor' all work together, that everyone takes account of what is going on and recog-nises that they all depend on each other.

I found this lesson very useful later in my career in France, when I was faced with a very hostile situation. I made sure then that I was seen to be around on the shop floor and showing an interest in what everyone did. I did this for two reasons: the first is that you can learn a great deal from people who are actually doing the work, and the second is that it is very important to maintain contact with everyone, so that you don't create or make worse, a 'them and us' situation.

*

Even having seen what went on at Lucas, the experience of office life just made me hungrier to get out and kick-start my career. I'm often asked whether I had a blueprint or a plan when I set out. The short answer is 'no'. I wanted to prove myself and feel good about myself – as the French say, '*bien dans ma peau*' (good in my skin).

With my parents, graduating from an MBA course in 1990.

The opportunity to enter the family business was also there, but I just could not see myself fitting in. The simple fact is that I realised that, while I enjoyed working in business (any kind of business – it didn't matter to me), I felt most comfortable in an office environment. I worked as a filing clerk during one summer holiday and I loved it! (They offered me a job at the end of the holidays because I had been such a good worker.) And this is something I tell people now, when they ask me about how to be successful: do everything you can, as well as you can. If you're stacking shelves in a supermarket, be the best you can be at it. There are always opportunities for those who are diligent and show ability.

When I completed my degree, Lucas CAV gave me one such opportunity: they offered me a permanent position. But there was no way on earth I was going to stay on at that godforsaken place. Instead, I had a lucky break. I had applied for various jobs advertised in the papers, one of which was for Batchelors foods in Sheffield. I didn't know too much about them; it was just one of my many applications for a graduate position.

After hearing nothing following my application, I called them and they said the vacancy had been filled, but they explained that they were part of Unilever, and suggested I get in touch with a man called Rodney Newth. He was based at Unilever's head office in Blackfriars (a striking art deco building where they are still headquartered today) and he was looking for someone. There and then I rang, and he asked me to come for an interview. We got on well, and it turned out that I had pretty much landed the job before I even walked in, because he was under pressure to fill the vacancy. I didn't learn my interview technique from Rodney Newth – something *The Apprentice* candidates probably regret!

Rodney was a graduate and an accountant, and he was pleased when I explained to him that I wanted to finish off my accountancy exams, as I only had one set of papers left in order to qualify. I was delighted when I received the letter confirming my appointment as the management accountant for chemicals co-ordination, working in the Finance Group.

The salary was significantly higher than that offered to me by Lucas CAV and, more importantly, this role held the promise of a career with a world-class company.

Unfortunately, the manager I was replacing was leaving pretty quickly, so I only had a couple of weeks' handover – not enough to fill the gaps in my knowledge of what the job entailed, or how to actually do it. I had learned about accounting in theory, but had zero experience of what the numbers actually meant.

In any business, the financials have to be interpreted, and appropriate actions can then be taken in conjunction with other salient information. I was saved by two Sri Lankan accountants. One of them in particular, called Udi Tennekoon, helped me enormously and, together with Gamit Ameresekere, pretty much did my work for three months, while I did my best to get to grips with what was required. It's an incredibly important lesson – perhaps a really obvious one – but to be an effective accountant you need to understand the business itself. So I had a crash course in what the division did, how to prepare and present the monthly accounts, and how to understand the significance of the numbers. This last part enabled me to write an analysis of the state of the business and what was going on.

Having analysed the management information received from each subsidiary in the Chemicals Division and collated the information in my report, I would pass my pack upstairs, to a department called simply 'Co-ordination'. To a mere twenty-three-year-old on my pay grade, these people were like gods! For a start, they sat on the same floor as the main board director for chemical co-ordination, Mr Ronnie Del Mar.

I always used to give my pack to Mr Del Mar's sidekick, John Reid. He was a very senior manager but terribly disorganised. He was Scottish and had a catchphrase if he couldn't locate a piece of paper, which was most of the time: 'Oh, the gremlins have got it.'

I still think of that whenever I can't find something, and often murmur those words in a Scottish accent!

Once I'd got the hang of the job, I spent a lot of time upstairs with John and, because of that, I came under the watchful eye of Mr Del Mar and some of the other senior managers on that floor. This turned out to be useful, since I would never have come into contact with anyone so senior if I'd stayed on my own floor all the time.

I absolutely worked myself ragged once I understood what I was doing. I really did – I did the best I could. Sometimes John would ask me to write the main report and I'd do it with pride. It didn't matter to me how long it took; all I was focused on was improving my understanding of the business and doing a good job. After a while, Udi and Gamit started to poke fun at me for spending so much time in Co-ordination – busy, as they saw it, blatantly 'brown nosing'.

Despite the fact that Unilever really was a superb company, the conditions weren't ideal. This was the beginning of 1974 and the Three-Day Week was in full swing: the government had imposed a shorter week to ration power because the coal workers were on strike and power stations were therefore producing much less electricity. I remember being given candles so that we could continue working once the lights had been switched off! If that wasn't enough, there was no heating either, so we'd be sitting there in our coats, shivering over our ledgers. It's strange to think of those times, now that we seem to take so much for granted.

We were all keen to work, but Unilever eventually realised that nothing very useful was coming out of those 'dark periods', so we, like everyone else working in the country, were sent home. The fact that we tried to carry on, though, I think, shows how dedicated we were.

After about a year, I spoke to Rodney during my annual review. He was very complimentary about my performance and I took the opportunity to say that I'd like to be promoted to a managerial grade. He said, 'Oh I don't know . . . I'll have to speak to John.' Of course, John agreed and I became a manager. I was so happy that I had risen through the ranks very quickly. I was on a fast track.

I got on well with John, so senior people didn't have a bad word to say about me. And Rodney supported me as his prodigy. But I was also putting in the hours and never ever missing a deadline. That would have been inexcusable. The fact is that, within that environment, everyone worked hard – that was the culture. Where Lucas CAV was a deplorable company, Unilever was an excellent one: really well organised and integrated, with all the parts of the business working in unison.

The contrast between the two companies very much struck a chord with me. Unilever was a distinguished company offering a real career path, with very clever, knowledgeable and dedicated people and none of the petty silliness, outdated systems and poor management practices that I experienced at Lucas CAV. I'd gone from the ridiculous to the sublime.

As time went on, I was given more and more responsibility, such as travelling to the subsidiaries to meet with the chief accountants and finance directors to get a better understanding of their business, the industry and the future financial outlook. The role continually increased in scope.

After a while, I got a call from Lord Tom Trenchard, who was the main board director for Meat Products Co-ordination, offering me a position in his team: commercial manager, meat products co-ordination – a similar role to that held by John in Chemicals Co-ordination. If ever the saying 'It is *who* you know, rather than *what* you know' was true, it was for me in getting that job. My mates at Chemicals Co-ordination must have put in a good word – or two!

I seized the opportunity. I was not quite Lord Trenchard's right-hand man, as there was a very senior manager between us, but very close to it. It was a fantastic position in an important division of the company, not profitable, but large and significant. Walls, Lawsons, Mattesons and Unox were all big Unilever-owned meat brands.

The job was a good promotion and, for a twenty-six-year-old, the prestige and salary increase were very appealing. I got a big office (with a carpet that fitted right to the edge – a status symbol at the time, and one only afforded to senior managers) that was only one office away from Lord Trenchard. Such status symbols might all be nonsense, but it was motivating at the time. It really was.

Also, instead of having to send my letters to the typing pool, I had a secretary who would take down my words in shorthand. The trouble was that I was incapable of dictating what I wanted to say, and made countless corrections to my letters. One day she ended up in tears because I made her redo a letter so many times.

Lord Trenchard was an English gentleman. He was often out of the office, travelling to the companies within the group or to the House of Lords. The person I reported to – the one in the office between me and Lord Trenchard – was called Smokey Eades. He had been in the meat business all his life and he was an expert. He knew everything and everyone. He was one of those people whom you meet in big companies who are indispensable. And I set out to find out as much from him as I could. Even then, I recognised that there is no substitute for knowing your business inside out, regardless of your role. And if you don't know it, then surround yourself with people who do!

Smokey was a senior manager, of course, an old-timer who wasn't going anywhere, but he played a vital role because of his knowledge. He didn't do much work at that point. In fact, when Lord Trenchard was away, he would call me into his office to show me his extensive coin collection, discuss his latest share purchases, or outline the finer points of croquet, in which he had a passionate interest. Notwithstanding all that, Lord Trenchard relied on him very heavily for key industry decisions, and Smokey was a really engaging character.

In spite of Smokey's expertise, however, the Meat Division was in trouble: it was loss-making and Lord Trenchard was under pressure from his board colleagues to turn it around. As I understood it, he had accepted the challenge of a turnaround within twelve months, or he would resign. We had a frantic year, but, at the end of it, the meat business was still in trouble and Lord Trenchard resigned. That left me exposed, because I had no real experience or in-depth knowledge of the business. A new boss came in, a Dutchman, and I didn't have any rapport with him. Also, he must have looked at Smokey and thought, That's no good. He's an old fart. But his knowledge was invaluable so they couldn't let him go.

I was enjoying my career at Unilever and doing really well. I was happy and thought I had opportunities ahead of me. But these developments spelled the beginning of the end – as a change of leadership often does. Within a few months, two new heavyweight senior managers, Brian Andrews and Paul Preston, were brought in to beef up the team.

I, meanwhile, became superfluous, with Paul pretty much taking over my responsibilities and Brian offering me 'wonderful career opportunities' in far-flung offices with no prospects, all of which I refused. I also declined a move back to the Finance Department, despite the assurance that I would retain my elevated pay grade. Unilever couldn't make me redundant – there were no grounds – but I effectively had no job. I knew that, when my annual review came up, there would be no bonus, no pay rise and certainly no promotion. By this time, I was married and had a young family. I was stuck.

The writing was on the wall and I knew I was going to have to find another job. I set about looking for one while I was still 'employed' at Unilever. My father once again suggested I join the family business, but I just couldn't bring myself to say 'yes'. (If there is an easy and a difficult way to do things, I always seem to take the difficult route. I don't make things easy for myself.)

I just wanted to do it on my own. I wanted to be

independent. I did know, however, that I was never going to be out on the street: if it came to it, I knew my father would help, but I really didn't want that.

*

Unilever and Lucas CAV were my first experiences of large corporate companies, and they couldn't have been more different: Lucas was stuck in the Dark Ages, while Unilever was at the forefront of product development and marketing.

I was, and remain, full of admiration for Unilever. I spent seven unforgettable years there and worked with some brilliant people who went on to achieve great careers within Unilever and other FTSE 100 companies. Paul Preston, my nemesis at the time, went on to achieve great things at Unilever and, as it happens, has become a good friend.

I think the experience brought something home to me, however: if a fantastic company like Unilever couldn't find a role for me, perhaps I was far more suited to doing things for myself. Now, at the age of thirty, I was about to find out what starting my own company was all about.

A good idea

Working for myself for the first time taught me a lot about the real world, about how desperately hard it can be to make a living in business – how to make a profit, to have your wits about you, to cope with disappointments and bounce back from setbacks. It taught me to persevere when your offers and deals are repeatedly declined and how to handle staff who let you down – all the while carrying the weight of responsibility. It was rough, tough and challenging – and I loved it.

Midway through 1979 I was still treading water at Unilever. It was frustrating and I was anxious to find something new. As it happened, my brother-in-law had started a business with a couple of partners, one of whom, David, was a bit of a wheeler dealer. I met him and asked if, when he came across any businesses he intended to invest in, perhaps he might keep me in mind as I was looking for an opportunity. 'Yeah,' he said, 'as a matter of fact I am looking at a paper company next week and perhaps you could go and take a look at it and write a report on it for me. If I decide to buy it, maybe you could run it for me.'

So I went along, wrote the report, and David's response was: 'Yeah, sounds interesting, but I don't fancy it.' Okay. A couple of weeks went by and I called again. He sent me off to look at another company – women's accessories this time. I wrote the report. Same answer.

This went on for some months with no joy, until one day he called me up. 'Look, probably of no interest, but I am meeting a director of Burton Menswear [the high street men's fashion shop] at my office and I was thinking you might like to come along and sit in on the meeting.' I agreed once again – after all, what did I have to lose? I was duly introduced to Tony Colman, a main board director of Burton Group.

This was the late seventies when the UK economy was in the pits, recovering from the miners' strike and the Three-Day Week, and Burton Menswear was not doing well in this challenging environment. Its shops were dowdy, and the whole of its estate needed refurbishment. Significant investment had been made in other parts of the Burton Group, such as Topshop, Dorothy Perkins and some newer fascias, but Burton Menswear was in the doldrums.

Burton had decided that, in order to revitalise their stores, they needed a large capital expenditure budget, and that left them very short of money to buy new stock. Their solution was to introduce the novel concept (at the time) of concessions – 'shops in shops' – and Tony Colman was the man who was going to make it happen. This spelled good news for branded manufacturers who had long been very keen to get their stock into Burton's, but had had few orders placed.

Tony was focused on finding manufacturers who were prepared to stock their stores on a concession arrangement, and that was of interest to David, as he had a leather company that could manufacture belts for Burton. However, as the meeting progressed, it became clear that it was going nowhere: David insisted on having exclusivity for belts and Tony could not accept that, because they had their own branded belts. This was a deal-breaker. So that was that – stuck again.

Trudging back to my non-job at Unilever, I mulled the situation over. I wouldn't have minded being non-exclusive, I thought. After all, I had no other options at the time. So I phoned David to ask whether he was planning on taking the discussion any further. He wasn't, so I asked whether he would mind me trying to work something out myself. 'Do what you like, Claude' was the response.

The next day, I arranged to meet Tony Colman at Burton's head office, above Topshop in Regent Street. That meeting changed the course of my life. Tony appeared as desperate to get concessions into Burton as I was to get myself out of Unilever. He said, 'Look, Claude, I am looking to place concessions in our shops. Our commitment is to refurbish our stores and create a modern look and feel, and concessions will stock our stores and bring in exciting, fresh, branded ranges over a broad product category. I am particularly looking for someone who can put together a range of menswear accessories. Belts, socks, ties, underwear and small leather goods – that sort of thing. Do you think you can do that?'

My heart was racing, my brain was in overload. Of course I couldn't. What are you on about? I haven't a clue!

So naturally I said, 'Yes, of course I can' ... I can't say no to a challenge!

'In that case, I'll do what I can to help you. I will write a letter on Burton's headed notepaper, signed by me, a main board director, that states that you are authorised to provide menswear accessory concessions within the Burton Group on an exclusive basis.' I knew that that piece of paper would be like dynamite and could open a lot of doors with menswear accessory manufacturers.

There were only two very tiny obstacles to exploiting this opportunity of a lifetime: I had absolutely no contacts in menswear accessories and, of even greater concern, I did not have the finance to support the working capital. In short, even if I found a manufacturer who was interested, I couldn't afford to buy the stock!

I was so near to starting something, and yet it remained so very far away. It was frustrating. How can I make this work? No one was going to sell me stock on credit – why would they? So I was stuck again, on two fronts: how was I going to find the stock, and how could I fund it once I did?

The awkward situation at Unilever was intensifying. By this time, I had been eased even further out of my job and had nothing to do. In effect, I was on gardening leave, so at least I was free to try and find a solution to these problems and exploit this seemingly wonderful opportunity. There was a menswear exhibition in London at that time, and I went along and approached various manufacturers. Many would not even allow me on their stand, because I was not an established retailer. I was reduced to collecting business cards and publicity material from the exhibitors' stands with the intention of contacting them later.

Going to the fair must have started a process in my mind, because now I did have an idea. It dawned on me that manufacturers are not retailers, and could not be seen to be acting as retailers, as that would undermine their retail customers, whom they depended on for their existence. The retailers would shut them out in an instant.

Burton, for their part, would not be buying branded stock, because they had their own production facilities and brands to support, and were putting capital expenditure into smartening up their fascias. What was needed was a 'consolidator' or enabler, to manage the process of manufacturers directly engaging in retail. So, I thought, maybe I could facilitate that coming together by placing myself as the middleman, aiming to stock the Burton shops with merchandise and to manage that stock for the manufacturers. It was a wonderful eureka moment.

My resulting proposal to the manufacturers was simple, or, at least, I attempted to make it simple. Let's say a pair of socks was retailing for £2.50. In a normal trading arrangement, I'd have bought them for £1 from the manufacturer, doubled up the price and added VAT. However, that would have required cash, which I didn't have, so instead I concocted an arrangement whereby the manufacturers would supply me with, say, twenty dozen pairs of socks for free, and as and when those socks were sold, I'd pay them the full wholesale price (£1) plus a split of the retail profits. So, provided they were confident I wasn't going to do a runner with their stock, this deal meant they could have stock in Burton's, receive the wholesale price for that stock, and make some money on top when the stock sold. Their position as manufacturers would not be compromised, I didn't have to find funding, and the business would be scalable to boot. Perfect.

With this structure in mind, towards the latter part of 1979 I approached a number of the manufacturers whose business cards I had picked up, or whom I had met, at the menswear exhibition. Many said 'no', because they didn't like the idea of parting with stock without raising an invoice, as well as not getting paid within their terms and conditions. However, a sock company called Byford Socks in Leicester was prepared to give it a try. With Byford on board, I managed to attract a number of others. I now had something to sell and, having spoken to Tony Colman, was given my first concession site, which was in Southampton. By the time I got it underway, I had a belt and tie manufacturer on board as well. A nice little range!

There are two further points about this deal that pleased me. The first was that it was profitable for me from week one. There was no cash investment, very low overheads, and I paid Burton eighteen per cent of my turnover, so there was enough margin on sales for me to pay the manufacturers their full trade price, and give them the agreed share of the retail margin.

The second point was that, although I knew nothing about men's accessories, I managed to get the manufacturers to supply me with their current and bestselling ranges. How did I do that? Well, I simply said to them, 'In this business model, everything depends on me being able to sell the stock you supply. So, if you give me old or redundant stock, I won't be able to sell it and you'll get it back – and that won't be good for either of us. Supply me with the good stuff, and I'll sell it.' So I got the good stuff – and it worked.

Of course, on the margins I was making I couldn't afford to take anyone on to run the concession. So, I spoke to the manager in Southampton and asked him whether it would be possible for one of his staff to keep an eye out for customers in my section, serve them and, when an item was sold, make sure my sales ticket was placed in a specific box, so that I was able to account for the sales to the various manufacturers. He agreed and the system worked well. I probably took just a couple of hundred pounds during the first few weeks, but I got the hang of replenishing stock and introducing new man-ufacturers and there was a steady increase week on week in turnover. The branch manager was happy, the manufacturers were happy and I was in business.

Meanwhile, I had told Unilever what I was doing and, to their credit, they hadn't stopped me from pursuing it, despite having made it clear to me that they thought the venture would fail, and that they would take me back when it did. Now I was finally able to inform them that my fledgling business was making a profit. They could stop paying me and I would not be coming back. I was sad that my career at Unilever had come to such an end, but, by the same token, I had to look to the future.

With the Southampton operation going well, I urged Tony to let me put my concession in more branches. As a start-up company and one-man band, I suggested that per-haps I could expand to create a network on the south coast. Tony offered me Derby. I took it anyway and, after Derby, I got space in the Nottingham shop. One by one, I grew my network of concessions, and, around six months later, the business was beginning to look reasonably healthy.

As in most industries, there are Key Performance Indicators (KPIs). These are essentially yardsticks by which performance can be evaluated and measured. In retail, one of these KPIs is sales per square foot. This is a good measure of how efficiently you are using the sales space. In the Burton Group, each store manager was given a minimum sales target per square foot, and this was measured on a weekly basis. Concessions were treated in the same way: we all had to 'earn our space' within the store, or we were relegated to a less valuable area in the store, or told by the manager to vacate.

I was in a fortunate position because, although ties and belts were sold by Burton as an own-brand range alongside mine, it was important to offer a broad choice. In addition, a number of other items in my menswear accessory range were not carried by Burton. The key for Burton was that my range was yielding a minimum sales per square foot, and that I could provide a range of menswear accessories for each branch offered, while managing the logistics.

Around this time, Burton gave me a space in their Oxford Street branch, right opposite Selfridges. That was a fantastic store, because of its very high footfall. It had a narrow shop front and they set me up right by the front door. For that store, I introduced a range of branded suitcases and holdalls, in addition to my standard accessory package, as it was obvious that this would attract the tourist trade on Oxford Street.

The manager of the store, Jim, was a Scotsman who was determined to make his branch the highest turnover store per square foot in the Burton Group. I was doing unbelievable business there; it was my best concession by a long way. In fact, my turnover in the Oxford Street store was higher than all the other concessions I had at that time put together, even though, very frustratingly, I did lose stock to shoplifting.

I got quite friendly with Jim and one day he said to me, 'I have a shop assistant called Lorraine and she is outstanding at sales. If you put Lorraine into your concession, your sales will double. She is that good.'

'I'm sure you are right,' I said, 'but I just can't afford to take on staff at this stage.'

'Look,' he said, 'I'll tell you what I'll do. You don't have to pay her a penny but I will put Lorraine on to your concession for a couple of weeks, and let's look at the results after that.'

So, Lorraine sold my merchandise and, sure enough, sales went through the roof. In addition, she was very good at paperwork and, on her days off, she would come to my office, count up all the tickets, complete all the manufacturer returns and do pretty well everything else. She absolutely transformed my business, and eventually became my first full-time employee, coming up with a host of great ideas for enhancing the concessions, introducing new accessories and displaying the items to attract customers.

This was important to me for three reasons: the first was psychological – hiring my first employee was a big step forward for my business. Second, I had had to evaluate whether she would be able to increase sales, week in week out, enough to make employing her a sound investment and help the company grow. The third was that I realised she was a real asset, as she brought knowledge of the products and retail experience that I simply didn't have.

With my Burton concessions doing well, and the addition of new branches on a regular basis – including Tottenham Court Road and the flagship Regent Street store – my father, quite by chance, spotted in the newspapers an advert placed by the old-fashioned department store Bourne & Hollingsworth on Oxford Street, near Oxford Circus.

The store had just been acquired by the Raybeck Group – a real go-getting fashion group that had big plans for the store. They had already changed the name to simply 'Bournes' and wanted to create a lively, modern, American-style buzz in the store with lots of different concessions. I was there the very next day, meeting with Andrew Bailey and Peter Ansel, the new store directors.

Once the pair had visited my concessions in Burton, the deal was done very quickly. Within a few weeks, I was trading in Bournes with my extensive menswear accessory package: gloves, socks, ties, scarves, underwear, pyjamas, and a range of cufflinks and small leather goods. The stock was slightly more upmarket – Pierre Cardin was one of the brands, and HOM underwear – and I was the only concession selling these products within the department store. Even better, I had my own dedicated area in the store, just as you walked in from the Wells Street entrance. It was a perfect location with high footfall and visibility.

There was a buzz around Bournes – almost every day they put on events and shows for shoppers. They used celebrities and managed to generate real excitement. It was all very innovative – for the early 1980s! At Christmas my tills were overflowing with cash, and I was getting Security to empty them every hour. Everything was selling, and I could barely keep up with the volume, stock ticketing and replenishment.

I still wasn't buying – I was using the same formula with manufacturers I had at Burton and it worked well.

Business was booming for me. I had grown to around fifty concessions, and there were some new opportunities presenting themselves in Bournes. An early one came about when a rival shirt concession there decided to pull out, because, for whatever reason, it just wasn't working for them. As that concession was next to mine, between my stand and the Wells Street entrance, I spoke with Peter Ansel about it. 'I can do it' became my mantra, and Peter told me I could give it a go.

At the time 'pilot' shirts with epaulettes were very popular, and I found a cash-and-carry wholesaler in Great Eastern Street who supplied these. They would not entertain my 'scheme', so, for the first time, I actually had to buy the shirts and pay money upfront, but it was worth it. The moment I put them on the shop floor, they flew out. I was onto a winner! My prices were right and it worked. I couldn't run to the wholesaler fast enough to replenish the stock.

Things continued to go brilliantly, until I popped into Bournes one day at lunchtime and saw that all the shirts had gone. I thought we'd had a fantastic morning and that I'd better hurry up and pick up some more stock, but then John, my shop manager, dropped the bombshell. All the shirts had been stolen and he hadn't been able to prevent it, because he'd been looking after the accessory concession and was distracted. He couldn't be in two places at once.

Okay, I thought, lesson to be learned here. I had been too stingy: I had cut my expenses to the bone, not taken on someone extra to cover the new concession and now

I had paid the price. It was heart-breaking. I had done everything on a shoestring and eventually the shoestring had snapped.

I immediately employed someone – a young man called Lawrence. Both John and Lawrence were very loyal and hard-working and this left me free to get on with the ticketing and pricing in a hot, stuffy, windowless stockroom in the basement of Bournes. I spent hours and hours down there, coding, pricing and ticketing every item of stock. My hands would be raw and bloodied from occasionally stabbing myself with the ticketing gun. I wanted to make sure that the guys on the shop floor could just concentrate on selling and keeping an eye on the stock.

One of the things that start-ups need to be acutely aware of is that you have to do whatever it takes. It's not just about being the boss and expecting the money to come rolling in – you have to really get stuck in, understand the fundamentals of the business, while all the while thinking ahead and keeping track of sales, margins and overheads.

Bournes was sensational for me. My concessions were well positioned and that meant there was always great footfall – and I had the right goods at the right prices. In my own modest way, I continued to expand, taking on a vacated sportswear concession and the childrenswear department on the first floor. Eventually, when Allied Carpets moved out, leaving all their fixtures, fittings and waterfall displays, I took over the top floor with a carpet and rug concession, supplied on sale or return from my father's company. It was easy and lucrative as I just 'piggybacked' on his operation with carpet fitters and delivery vans.

Bournes, however, were beginning to realise that the

new department store concept was not working out to be the goldmine they thought it would. Their gamble on transforming Bourne & Hollingsworth wasn't paying off and further concessions were opting out. They eventually announced that they were going to close down. However, they did not actually say when . . .

The sale signs went up – and stayed up – drawing a significant increase in bargain-hunting shoppers. For the next two years or so my turnover was spectacular, as I now encouraged my suppliers to give me all the old stock they had, so I could sell it at very low prices and generate high sales.

Meanwhile, the Burton fascia had become a much stronger proposition on the high street. They had succeeded in greatly improving their image. Tony Colman had done an outstanding job of attracting concessions and these had inevitably provided Burton with a detailed understanding of the broad range of merchandise their customers wanted, as well as their profile on a store-by-store basis.

I could anticipate what that would mean for me: Burton would no longer need the concessions. It started in the Oxford Street branch. They said to me that they were more than happy for me to continue my concession, but they were moving my position right to the back of the store. That was the kiss of death! Also, they upped the terms of the deal – whereas eighteen per cent of turnover went to Burton with staff available to oversee my concession, it would now be twenty-six per cent and staff I had to employ myself. Whereas, previously, store managers had been clamouring for my menswear accessory packages, they were now asking me to vacate. It was game over.

Eventually, Bournes closed as well, and that was the end of that lucrative and exciting chapter in my career.

*

It hadn't been a case of me seeking out that opportunity with Burton Group – it almost fell into my lap – but, when it happened, I understood the potential and took action. I grasped the opportunity, gave it my all and it paid off handsomely. It was a similar story, I think, with the concessions at Bournes and the way I had managed to seize every opportunity to expand that business. My motto throughout had been 'I can do it', and I did!

When it all finished, I had secured my family's future and felt that I could make anything work. I had got into retail through a mixture of opportunism and single-mindedness. But I think the word 'hubris' is appropriate for the next chapter of my career.

The School of Hard Knocks

There are myriad business lessons to be learned from the next stage of my career, and anyone reading this book would be right to come away thinking that if I had been a candidate on *The Apprentice*, I would have been fired at the very first opportunity!

My sportswear business at Bournes had done pretty well and, being a keen sportsperson myself, I thought I had some insight into the market. So I took this thought to its logical conclusion and decided that sports retail was a business I could really excel in. Buoyed by my success, I decided that, instead of paying a percentage of my sales to a host company, I'd acquire some shops myself. After all, I was 'the man', and pretty infallible, so it made absolute sense.

I approached Midland Bank Venture Capital (MBVC), which has since ceased to exist, and asked if they were interested in investing in my new business idea. Based on my previous success, a review of my accounts and my unwavering enthusiasm, they were keen to do so, and I issued convertible preference shares in the new entity, which meant MBVC had the option of transferring their loan into a twenty-five per cent stake in my company. They agreed to the terms, one of which was that they couldn't at any point in the future withdraw the investment.

I had identified three shops I wanted immediately, as well as a further three targets for acquisition in the second phase of my expansion – I was pretty damn optimistic! Having overcome my failure at school, I believed success was now part of my new DNA.

The first property was in a densely populated but not very affluent part of London. The site was an existing sports shop which had been established for a while on a really busy high street. A perfect location. However, from here on, I have omitted names and places to spare the blushes of everyone involved.

The owner wanted to sell, and I had reviewed his accounts and found the figures impressive. The leasehold on the premises was also reasonable and I was attracted by the fact that the property was on three floors and had a lift. The ground floor comprised the retail space with a small stockroom at the back and a parking space to the rear of the shop; the first floor had a large, well-fitted-out stockroom, and on the top floor was an area big enough to be used as a comfortable office.

My so-called due diligence consisted of looking at the accounts, spending a Saturday in the shop observing the footfall and scrutinising the till rolls at the end of the day. After a brief chat with the seller, we agreed to get an independent valuer in to assess the stock and agreed a price. What more did I need? I just wanted to get going.

I completed the deal and brought in staff, including John

from Bournes and some local part-timers. I wasn't down on the shop floor; I was upstairs in my office setting up meetings with sales reps and progressing my negotiations with the other two retail outlets I wanted to lease.

Sadly, it wasn't long before I realised I had been shafted – and that it was my own fault. Fifty per cent of the previous owner's turnover had been supplying schools with gymwear – shorts, plimsolls, gymslips and so on. The other fifty per cent was general retail from customers coming into the shop. The problem was that the owner did not relinquish his school supply business. So I was down fifty per cent on what I had calculated before I had even started.

I couldn't just set up a competing school supply business, because I didn't have the contacts or the contracts to do so. A proportion of the stock the independent valuer had assessed were odds and ends, and broken size ranges (missing key sizes) of the school supply contract business, which were virtually unsaleable. So, almost from week one, when I totted up the takings and compared them to the previous year's number, I knew I was in deep trouble.

I had looked at the seller's figures – he had supplied them all – but hadn't thought to ask even the most basic questions about the composition of the turnover. I hadn't scrutinised the stock, or included a non-compete clause. I had taken everything on trust. I had made a huge mistake. I wasn't happy, obviously, but no matter, I thought. I can do this. With my Midas touch, surely I would find a way of turning this around.

But I didn't. I couldn't.

Part of the problem was that I was out of my depth. The customers, for the most part, were young people who knew exactly what they were looking for. They wanted bang-up-to-the-moment branded fashion sports goods. 'Street cred' was all-important. But I didn't understand that culture. I wasn't connected. I had brought in a lot of unbranded stock from Bournes, which was useless to these discerning customers. This was compounded by the fact that the branded stock I had acquired as part of the purchase of the shop was in last season's colours – not that I could have told you that. Where I had a particular style of green Adidas trainers, they wanted the pink ones. So, I had almost entirely unsaleable stock.

My West End experience had also left me ill-prepared for being a retailer in this area. Customers would come in and look at a tracksuit, feel the fabric and say how much they liked it, but that there was a mark on it and they would only buy it at a discount. Now, they had smeared the mark on the sleeve themselves. I knew that, but what could I do? If I wanted to make the sale, I had to mark down the soiled item.

Fridays and Saturdays proved to be another eye-opener. Typically, we would sell a shedload of goods on those days. Wonderful . . . the shop was packed and buzzing. But, on the Monday, the shop would fill with customers demanding refunds on the partly worn items for a host of completely spurious reasons. These were not customers you could easily reason with!

Having become acutely aware of the problem fairly early, I knew I had to try and put things right quickly. So when, for example, the Nike rep came in, I ordered the latest styles in the most outrageous colours. I stocked them, and for the first few weeks or so they flew off the shelves and the customers were happy . . . but only for the first week or so; the week after that these colours and styles dropped out of fashion and I didn't have the next 'hot' item.

The key, if there was one, seemed to be to buy little and often, so you always had something new and fresh to offer. But, even armed with that knowledge, I still had no idea what was going to appeal to my customers.

I was dashing around the other local sports shops almost every day, doing trades for different sizes of shoes or shirts to make sure that I could make a sale. I was giving it everything, but making little headway. The contrast could not have been greater with my previous retail experience. At Burton and Bournes, I was not dealing in cutting-edge or street fashion. I was selling, by and large, staple items to a less demanding clientele. But here I was subjected to the vagaries of fashion and the whims of customers I didn't understand.

After a few months, the MBVC manager came to see me and although I made reassuring noises about the business, I no longer had the heart to embark on setting up further sports shops. Throughout my career I have depended on people who have an in-depth knowledge of their industry and business, leaving me able to focus on the commercial aspects, bringing in common sense and business acumen. In this situation, I had no one I could readily tap for advice.

Things only got worse from there. There was the time I received a phone call in the middle of the night from the police to tell me that there had been a break-in at the shop. I immediately bombed down there, and found that the thief had come in through the skylight. There was blood everywhere and a fair amount of stock had been stolen. I sat there guarding my shop all night. I have no idea what I would have done if the thief had come back with some of his mates!

Some months later, I got another call from the police. Another robbery. This time I didn't even go down – by then my heart had gone out of the venture. A week later, when I made my insurance claim, the insurance company informed me that they would pay me out on this occasion, but that my policy was now cancelled because it was too risky.

When the next season came around, and the Nike, Adidas and other reps came in to take my orders, I didn't bother to place a single one. My only thought was to exit from this nightmare. I had started contacting Domino's Pizza and other fast-food outlets, to see if they wanted to acquire the lease, but no one was interested.

By then John had moved on, but I still had some local part-time staff. I remember being up in the office one day when I glanced at the monitor feeding a view of the shop and noticed something odd going on. So I phoned downstairs to the shop assistant, to ask what was happening. 'We are being held up!' I quickly dialled 999, but by the time the police arrived, the robber had disappeared, having raided the till and rampaged through the shop, helping himself to stock. Unbelievably, the police caught up with the thief and hauled him back into the shop so that my shop assistant could identify him. He was still in possession of some of the stock. The police officers asked my shop assistant, 'Is this the man who robbed you?' Before she could answer, the thief said, 'If you say "yes", I'll be back to cut you.' I didn't blame her for a second when she shook her head and said it wasn't him. But it was another example of how impossible it was for me to operate successfully in such conditions. It was hopeless.

The business wasn't actually making a loss, but neither was it going anywhere. The issue was that it was never going to be a real success under my stewardship. I was drained and couldn't see a way out. So I decided to try to sell what I could, leaving whatever remained behind, and walk away from the shop, allowing the company to go under without any harm to anything except my reputation.

Then, literally two weeks before I had planned to close the door for good, I had the biggest stroke of luck I have ever experienced. I was on the shop floor when a burly bloke walked in and said, 'Are you the boss?'

For a moment I thought I was in trouble – another hold-up or something. What should I say? Yes? No? I hesitated and he said, 'You are, aren't you?' I didn't have much choice then: 'Yes.'

'Good. I want to buy your shop.'

'Why?' was all I could think of to say.

'I have a number of shops and businesses in this area. You have a prime position and I know how to make this place work. You are never going to make a go of it, but I know what the customers want. I know where to get the stuff. I am part of the community.

'Okay, that makes sense, but how?' I was still dumbstruck!

'I'll stock the ground floor with the latest fashion gear from the US. I know everything that people round here want. On the first floor, that will be drugs, and on the top floor, girls. I'm going to buy all your stock – the whole lot. Tell me the price and that's what I'll pay.'

You can imagine the sort of effect that this rather stunning plan had on me, but all I cared about was a way out of this hellhole. So we agreed a price and arranged to meet the following week at his solicitors' to sign the necessary paperwork.

We met as arranged, and after we were done with the documents, he handed over a briefcase. I opened it. Full of cash. I shut it quickly. 'Aren't you going to count it?' he asked.

'No, I am sure it's all there.'

I hurried down the narrow staircase that led out onto a busy street, dashed to the nearest bank, and deposited the money into the company account. And that was it. I contacted MBVC and repaid their loan in full, as well as the interest that had accrued.

*

Even now, I can't believe my luck. I had made a mistake and I had got away with it. I hadn't suffered a personal financial loss, but my confidence had been dented, that's for sure. What lessons had I learnt? I had been naive. I hadn't been careful enough. I had had too high an opinion of my ability, based on my previous successes, and I hadn't paid enough attention to the detail and the reality. I had taken it as read that I would make it work. I had spent a Saturday in a shop before I bought it and had seen how busy it was. I had thought that would be sufficient, together with checking the accounts. Well, it had been busy, and the accounts had pointed to a good business, but I should have understood the company, the customers, the stock and the location a lot better before I committed to it. There had been much more to it and I had barely scratched the surface.

When I had begun to understand the gravity of my mistake, and the simple truth that I couldn't rectify it, I had started to look around to see what I could do next. I had been beaten, but I wasn't broken. Time to pick myself up. I had learned a sharp and painful lesson from the School of Hard Knocks.

How do you say 'You're fired' ...
in French?

It would be easy to compare the next phase of my career with Amstrad, Tottenham, Powerleague, ASCO and *The Apprentice* and think it's all pretty mundane stuff, and in some ways it was. But, equally, at their heart, all commercial enterprises have the same guiding principle: you have to make a profit to survive – and, quite frankly, the sooner the better! And I am obsessed with business. Any kind of business. I just love the challenge – overcoming obstacles and finding solutions. I love the cut and thrust, the negotiating, the thrill of making a difference and, above all, winning ...

Nine months after taking over the sportswear shop, I responded to an ad in the newspaper (this was pre-internet after all) posted by a company asking for help in turning around businesses in the Midlands area. The man who ran the turnaround company – let's call him Turnaround Man – wanted help with one of the investments he had made in a business that serviced aircraft at Coventry Airport.

I went along, intrigued by the aircraft servicing business. It was really interesting: there was a huge warehouse full of aircraft parts, with technicians working on servicing planes. I thought it had the potential to be a really good business, but the company was dependent on a few key customers and the margins they were making did not take full account of the time it was taking to complete their work. They were in a loss-making position and pretty desperate. A good challenge, then! I was hooked and jumped straight in. The people were friendly, happy to explain their issues, and so appreciative of the work I was doing and the information I was providing.

One of the keys to managing a business is to maintain a tight control of overheads. I regarded the aircraft service company as a complex version of a local garage, and tried to establish how the business costed out its labour and materials. It was clear from the get-go that labour had an established, specific hourly cost/rate, but the Bill of Materials (BOM) was out of control. Engineers were using parts from the warehouse, but not recording them properly, nor including the cost of each part in the price they were charging the customer. There was also a breakdown in the process of ordering spare parts, so that they had quantities of old parts, but were always waiting for vital components that were on long lead times.

I got stuck in. However, after a few weeks, I smelt a rat. It looked very much like Turnaround Man was taking huge fees but actually providing no financial or institutional support. Things can work out like that sometimes: you just get an uncomfortable feeling that everything isn't as it should be and it leaves a sour taste in your mouth. Turnaround Man seemed to be in it for his own ends, rather than the good of the aircraft services business. I felt that I couldn't carry on, because it was going to end badly. I left that business with some regret, but also some relief.

As it happened, Turnaround Man was also involved with a local plumbing firm called Progress Plumbing in Leicester. John Wilson, one of the co-founders, had, over many years, built the business from nothing into a good, medium-sized company. The other co-owner had lost faith in the company's future and I acquired an option on his fifty per cent shareholding, because I saw it as a real opportunity.

The business was attractive to me as it looked like a pretty simple and straightforward operation. It was well established, but clearly needed shaking up, if John was anything to go by. He was a good man, wore a flat cap, and took great pride in keeping the bathroom and kitchen showroom spotlessly clean. Indeed, that seemed to be what he spent most of his time doing. He knew the plumbing business inside out, but was struggling with the day-to-day responsibility of running the company. He was always apprehensive about the threat of national plumbers' merchants opening up on his doorstep and killing his trade business, but he was well stocked and the tradesmen liked dealing with him. He was really a plumber at heart.

One of the problems was that John wasn't tough enough with suppliers, and then compounded the problem by being too generous with discounts to the trade and the public. As if that wasn't bad enough, he was also very poor at managing the credit control function, so the debtors' list was in bad shape. He just wasn't collecting money from his customers.

That was probably the reason why his partner had left. But I thought I could help turn things around. From my conversations with John, I sensed that he didn't trust Turnaround Man and, while he could see the value I was adding, he thought Turnaround Man was not helping at all. Sure enough, after I'd been there a short while, Turnaround Man was told not to return.

My first priority was to collect the overdue accounts. John was a simple man, but he was also quite obstinate, and I spent a lot of time trying to get him to negotiate tougher terms on purchases and to stay away from the customers, because he was a soft touch.

I set up a credit control department and recruited some YTS (Youth Training Scheme) people, and the team got down to phoning customers all day, every day, and getting commitments from them to pay. If payments did not materialise, I personally visited the customers at their homes and insisted on settlement. If that did not work, I issued County Court writs.

Within three months, we had collected almost all of the outstanding debts, provided copy invoices, and resolved genuine customer complaints that were holding up payments. We also tightened up our credit control procedures and established a 'stop' system if trade customers went over their agreed credit limits.

I worked with John to set up a simple model to ensure that he never sold bathrooms or kitchens in the showroom for below an absolute minimum price, which returned a satisfactory margin. But John could not help himself and was always offering extras free of charge in order to secure a deal. Despite this, within six months, Progress Plumbing was trading profitably and running quite nicely.

The company was a member of a trade association for

independent plumbing and heating merchants called AHED. When John's business first got into financial difficulties, it was AHED that took the unusual step of providing funding to protect it from the banks, who might have wanted to pull the plug – if you'll allow me the pun! AHED were serious business people who were effectively keeping Progress afloat through temporary funding; the objective was to allow the company the oxygen to get its house in order, and then repay the loans that AHED had provided.

Once I had cleaned up the business, and the company was back in profit, AHED realised that it would be a very long time before they got their loan and accrued interest paid back. I had some discussions with them and pointed out that, in effect, they controlled the company in all but name, and that perhaps they should consider buying it. They eventually agreed, because they were unlikely to get their money back any time soon. I discussed the deal at some length with John, who eventually agreed to relinquish control and sell his shares. I obtained an assurance from AHED that, post-acquisition, they would retain John in the business and agree to increase his salary.

Well, we got as far as sitting in front of the lawyer with the acquisition documents before us, when John turned to me and said, 'Claude, I'm sorry, but I just can't do it. I can't sell the business. It's my baby. I started it and I love it. I can't let it go.'

'John, listen, you've got to sell it. There is no other way out. We may be in the black, but the world is changing – there are bigger players out there who will take more and more business away from you. We may be okay now, but we are vulnerable to our bigger competitors. AHED are offering a great deal. You'll be earning forty per cent more than you are now. You'll have no worries, no risk of losing your house. You've got to take it.'

'I can't, Claude. I can't.'

'Listen to me, John. If you don't sign these papers today, then I am leaving and I am not coming back. You'll be on your own. This deal is your salvation!'

He would not budge. That was it. I walked out.

About six months later I saw a notice in the *Financial Times*. He'd gone bust. It was a great shame, but he just couldn't let it go – a problem I came to see with my own family's business, although it didn't have anywhere near as drastic consequences, of course.

The opportunity of getting stuck in at Progress Plumbing had been a very pleasurable one, all in all. The ultimate pay-off didn't happen, but the experience healed the wound of the sports shop debacle. I had enjoyed being at the coalface, collecting debts, scrutinising margins, getting better terms and turning the business from loss into profit. In other words, I had found the turnaround aspect of the whole experience very satisfying – not just transforming the fortunes of the company, but also redeploying employees to roles that suited them better and managing them to do the jobs they were paid to do. It was also gratifying to employ a couple of enthusiastic YTS people and see them prosper in the company.

*

If I hadn't exactly made a killing out of the Progress Plumbing venture, I'd seen a path forward. Turning companies around was something I could do, enjoyed doing and was good at. And so this plumbing firm marked the start of my career as a turnaround specialist and troubleshooter.

As part of my thinking about the future, when the sportswear shop was sinking, I had enrolled on an Executive MBA, which I felt would give me a leg up on the ladder to success. In any event, this was a qualification I had really aspired to and thought I would benefit from. After the sale of the sports shop, I became the retail director for a consultancy firm called Esprit. I had accepted this position as it allowed me time to finish my studies. However, working as a management consultant served to bring home the fact that I did not have the patience for that type of work. I'm not really interested in pontificating about how a company's business will be improved by 'x' per cent, or writing lengthy exposés on its performance, or lack thereof. Put simply, I want to get in, get on and fix it.

Then a job advertised in the newspaper really caught my attention. It was for a managing director to turn around a subsidiary of a public company, Renaissance Holdings plc. After numerous interviews with the group's managing director, the CEO and the chairman, I still hadn't been told the specifics of the role, the location of the business, the salary or even the industry. So I told them that I wasn't prepared to go for any more interviews until they disclosed the specifics, and made me an offer.

They did. They said that they had acquired, out of receivership, a ragbag of loss-making companies in France. In the first instance, they needed someone who was French-speaking to go in and turn around the fortunes of the biggest company in the group. I was dumbstruck. If they

had told me from the outset that I would be required to go
to France, I would have turned them down straight away
and saved everyone a lot of time.

CRISIS MANAGERS

RENAISSANCE HOLDINGS PLC, the expanding, special situation
and turnround Investment Trust, requires three experienced 'Crisis
Managers', to join its team of hands-on problem solvers.

YOUR RESPONSIBILITIES: To examine new projects and to take full
responsibility, usually for a period of six months each, for the turnround
of ailing companies, and to find and train replacement management.

OUR REQUIREMENTS: Creative, independent leaders who are
results-orientated performers, having the track record, the tenacity and
the human touch to make things happen in a shirt sleeve environment,
particularly in small to medium sized companies.

YOUR REWARDS: You will enjoy the fun of hard work, within a
stimulating collegiate environment; you will receive a high retainer for
being on call, and will receive generous rewards partially based on
results.

But where is the job?!

I did turn the job down, but they persisted. They
explained that they would be paying me a substantial salary,
that there would be performance bonuses and that they
were absolutely certain I was the man for them because of
my business experience and fluent French. They eventually
admitted they were desperate to get someone in and stem
the flow of losses.

The company they had earmarked for me was in
Cambrai, in the Nord-Pas-de-Calais, Northern France.
It was France's leading shirt manufacturer. I told them I
would go home and have a think about the offer, which I

did. Thelma, my wife, and I discussed it. I realised it was a brilliant opportunity, but the prospect of living away from home and being away from my family was unbearable. My children were at school at the time, so uprooting the family was a non-starter. Thelma then said, 'Why don't you give it a try? Go, see what you think, and if you don't like it, simple: come home.'

A week or so after that I was driving over to France with the group's chief executive, Richard Beamish. We stayed in a beautiful chateau on the first night and, over dinner, he said to me, 'Right, Claude, tomorrow we will get up at dawn and drive to the head office. The current chairman and chief executive who you will be replacing is a huge brute of a man – and I want you to go in and fire him!'

'Eh, hold on a second – you are saying I am meant to turn up out of the blue – he doesn't know who I am – and fire him on the spot. That's not going to work! *You* should fire him.'

'I can't fire him because I don't speak French. You do, so you fire him.'

That evening, lying in bed, I was quite unable to take in my surroundings, or get to sleep. There were several things on my mind, not least of which was that I didn't have a clue what 'You're fired' was in French. Yes, I spoke French well. But I had left the Lycée some twenty years ago and, apart from holidays in France, I hadn't really spoken the language since.

Early the following morning we drove to Cambrai, and Richard and I walked into the chairman's office. He was very surprised to see Richard, and I was astounded to see this monster of a man – he really was huge. I could feel my heart beating through my chest. The meeting was short and not very sweet. I blurted out something like *'Vous êtes . . . allez!'* (You are . . . going!) That's pretty much how it went.

The bloke went absolutely berserk, in a stereotypically French way, with lots of exaggerated gesturing and venting of emotion. He then went to leave and Richard jumped up from his seat and said to me, 'Quick, Claude, get the keys off him before he goes. That's going to be your car!' So I caught up with him just as he was getting into the car and told him to hand over the keys. He threw them on the driveway. I quickly picked them up and retreated to the office, where Richard bade me farewell and left me to it!

What the hell do I do now? I thought to myself. I was president directeur general of Les Trois Lords, sitting in a beautiful corner office overlooking fields, in the middle of I knew not where exactly. The situation was difficult, to say the least. The company was the main employer in the town and it didn't take long at all for word to get out that some English bloke had walked in and taken over.

Within moments of my confrontation with the now ex-chairman, there was a knock on my door, and in walked Daniel Leroux, the finance director. He was followed by the production director, Gerard Pereau, the sales director, Didier Kasperjak, the buying director and the fabric director. I wasn't sure what to expect, but I sat them down and explained the situation. To my astonishment, they were not at all hostile and welcomed me. Each of them took turns to explain their role in the company, the difficulty they had experienced working for their previous boss, and their commitment to working with me to turn the company around. It was a massive relief to have the support of the senior management team, and I remember thinking at the end of the meeting that there was a chink of light in the darkness.

Soon after the meeting broke up, a rather attractive woman popped into my office and, in a rather flirty way, asked me if there was anything she could do for me. It transpired that she was the previous boss's PA. I was quite enchanted at first as she ingratiated herself with me. But when I mentioned it to Daniel, the finance director, when he came into my office with all the management accounts and bank statements, he revealed that she was the ex-boss's mistress, and that her husband owned an upmarket shirt shop in the town. He then disclosed that she often stole shirts from the factory, unpicked the labels and replaced them with more upmarket labels. Her husband would then sell the relabelled shirts, passing them off as higher-quality, branded products. I couldn't believe it!

The previous boss knew what she was doing, but was hardly going to expose her. I decided that, with the co-operation of the senior management team, we would set a trap by installing a hidden camera. Sure enough, late one night, we caught her red-handed. Having since learned the French for 'You're fired,' the very next morning I told her, 'Vous êtes vire.'

This is where I had my first brush with French employ-ment law, because, according to legislation, you can't fire a 'protected' employee, which she was. By doing so, I had apparently almost committed an act of treason: the Bastille was my next stop!

I was required to present myself to the Town Hall and give my evidence to the mayor, who told me in no uncer-tain terms that I absolutely had to take the employee back, and merely issue 'madame' with a warning. I explained, in equally forthright terms, that I was not going to do that, and that if she was reinstated every single employee would walk out. Not strictly true, but she *was* very unpopular, and I did not think the mayor would find a walkout at the town's largest employer easy to defend. It took a while, but I won and the dismissal was allowed to stand. She never returned.

That bold move earned me a high degree of credibility and respect, not only among the office staff, but also in the factory that adjoined the office. And I knew that I had to continue to build on that if I was going to bring both with me in rescuing the company.

Meanwhile, I was still staying at the lovely Chateau de la Motte on the outskirts of the town. But it was expensive and I decided that I should not be seen to be living in luxury at great expense when the company was in trouble. So I got my new PA to book me into the local IBIS – a pretty basic hotel chain – where I stayed during the week. It was grim and cheerless. I hated it, but at least I felt that I was making an attempt to economise – leading by example, if in a small and frankly insignificant way.

The company was loss-making and it was obvious that we had to restructure in order to survive. I had made up my mind that the solution was simple. To turn the company around, I needed to engineer a situation whereby only the high-end branded shirts we manufactured under licence, and under our own 'Lords' label, would be manufactured in France, as these could command a premium price in the marketplace. The low- and possibly some mid-range shirts would need to be manufactured in the Far East or some other lower-wage economy.

I called a meeting with the management team to try and work out with them how we were going to implement the solution. This was a new experience for them, as previously they had just been told what to do. They had never been asked for their view, or to act in a collaborative way. The French are very respectful of hierarchy, but they immediately warmed to my new approach.

This process worked well for me, as I was on a steep learning curve and felt that the team really understood their products, and that the market was all working for the good of the company. We had three big factories and it soon became clear that we would have to close at least one of them – an incredibly difficult move given the strength of the unions in France. They were militant, obstructive and very hard to reason with.

Obviously the production director, Gerard, did not want to lose a single factory worker – let alone one or two whole factories! He redoubled his efforts to get better yields from the two factories under threat by bringing in *'negoce'* – third-party production during the quieter times – and did everything to keep the capacity up. Despite these steps, it was clear we had to close one factory and find a manufacturing outlet outside France to make our cheap ranges of shirts. We found two: one in Czechoslovakia and one in Bangladesh.

The proposed changes required a lot of hard work to keep the people in the factory onside. Although I had made my mark at the very start with the instant dismissal of the 'thief', there was a good deal of mistrust between management and factory. My daily walkabout on the factory floor, speaking to workers on the machines, was helpful, but naturally there was vehement opposition to my plan. However, at least I was not hiding; I was visible, approachable and listening to staff, and that really helped.

This picture of me confronted by union members in my office appeared in the newspaper *La Voix*.

After six months of negotiating on a daily basis with the unions, their representatives and their lawyers, the unions agreed to close one factory, but only on the condition that there would be no further closures, and that there would be a programme of investment in the latest technology in the remaining factories to cut down the time it was taking to make the shirts. If I did this, it would ensure that the company moved into profit, survived and grew (which was fine). So we had a hard-fought deal.

We also agreed to invest over a million pounds in

television advertising to promote our French-manufactured 'Lords' brand and raise our profile in the market. That also encouraged the unions to understand that we were not abandoning the French marketplace. They could see we were investing in France and looking at ways to improve sales, and therefore the company's prospects.

If we hadn't taken these steps, we would eventually have had to close all three factories. The unions did understand that, but as union representatives they had to do their utmost to preserve their workers' rights and employment.

Having to make all those factory staff redundant was very hard, but Gerard Pereau took care of that for me. He viewed the staff as his people and saw it as his responsibility to deal with the pain of the closure. The workers trusted Gerard; he was an honourable man and they knew that he would do the best he could for them, which he absolutely did.

Again, there was a huge difference between what I was doing in France and the awful job I had had in Lucas CAV. We needed to lay off those people in France; it was horrible, but it was necessary, or many more people would have lost their jobs as well. At Lucas, it seemed they just decided arbitrarily that they wanted to shed staff, then went out of their way to come up with a reason, rather than contemplate other viable options. What we were doing was at least fair. I think people did understand that.

I negotiated the price of the shirts to be manufactured outside France, and Gerard sent our production people to Czechoslovakia and Bangladesh to oversee the process until we were satisfied with the product. Finally, Didier, the sales director, was in a position to offer shirts to the very large hypermarkets at 'sacrificial' prices, safe in the knowledge that we were actually making a very acceptable margin.

The advertising campaign, and a more focused approach on the high-end, branded and 'manufactured in France' range, meant that our French factories were at full capacity, which pleased Gerard and the factory workers, who took great pride in manufacturing high-quality shirts.

Throughout this process, I had kept the UK investment company fully appraised of the difficult union negotiations, my future plans and finally the agreement that had been reached.

Things began to go well in France: the company was profitable and we initiated a programme of introducing the promised new equipment into the factories.

A mini head office was set up to oversee the ragbag of companies acquired in Northern France by the UK investment company. This activity was headed up by John Ward, who had been the managing director of Tootal, a UK shirt manufacturer. He became the chief executive of the French group – my boss in effect – and things started to go wrong. Badly wrong.

John and his new entourage lived in the lap of luxury in a country manor at St Omer, which the company had bought. I was summoned to present my results and give an update on the progress of the company. John would say things like, 'Claude, pop in and see me on Sunday, will you?' My response would be: 'No, sorry, I won't. I am home at the weekends.'

At board meetings, attended by all the companies within the French group, John would propose things that I felt were plain stupid. I would forcefully object, and he would respond with 'Respect for the chair!', to which I would counter, 'I can't respect the chair if the chair talks rubbish.'

I vented my frustration and emotion at him, in front of everyone. It seemed to me that the company had recruited wallies to run the other companies in France, all of which were struggling badly. Mine was the only one turning a profit, so I felt I had the strength of my results to fall back on. Quite frankly, I felt that he and the rest of his team were a complete waste of space, and that the country manor was an embarrassing waste of money.

After a while, John and his cronies were saying, 'Claude, your company is making good profit – real cash – and what we want to do now is to divert some of that cash into the other ailing companies.'

'Absolutely not. No way,' I yelled at him. 'As you know, I have given my word to the unions that we would invest in the shirt business. And that was the only reason they agreed to one of the factories closing. I have spent months and months negotiating for this position and I am not going back on it. If you have problems with those other companies, you fix them. Do not bleed my company to prop up the other ones. I won't allow it.'

John remained composed throughout, while I was losing it with him. 'We understand your position, Claude. We really do. But we are in a bind. The UK public company has no more money and they have asked me to sort out all these companies. You have the cash and we need that cash to give oxygen to the others.'

I refused to co-operate, but the next month the monies were withdrawn from the company bank account anyway.

Daniel, the finance director, was almost in tears, and Gerard was beyond consoling. 'You do realise, Claude, that if the unions find out about this, our lives will not be worth living. There will be a walkout and we will have breached our undertaking.'

'I know, but what can I do?'

It happened again in the second month, and I vented my fury at John. I stated quite clearly that if the money was diverted the following month, I would leave. I couldn't look people in the eye. Things were really heating up, and one evening I received an anonymous phone call telling me quite clearly not to get in my car. I don't think it was a hoax. I don't know who it was, and I don't know what, if anything, had been done to my car, but by now the unions were aware of what was happening and they must have been beside themselves with anger.

Inevitably, the money was withdrawn for a third time and I felt that I had no choice. I left the company. From my perspective, what was happening was badly misguided. The UK investment company had made a mistake in putting in place a pointless top-heavy structure. They also wanted to ride roughshod over everything that had been achieved in the shirt business. It was short-sighted and wrong.

*

With the benefit of hindsight, I can now appreciate the difficult situation that John Ward had been put in. Apart from raiding my company's funds, he apparently had no other means of trying to buy time to turn around the other loss-making entities. However, it's difficult to be anything other than dismissive about the way the managing company dealt with the problems in the group; it was blinkered, ill-considered and uncommercial. For me, though, the way my first French adventure ended at least allowed me to walk away with my head held high: I had realised I was very good at what I did and had accomplished a great deal. Success, I thought, was written all over my CV and ran through my veins.

The whole experience had been enlightening and, in retrospect, very enjoyable. The atmosphere in the company had been collaborative and positive, both in the management team and in the factory. I also felt that I had made a big difference. In difficult and stressful situations, strong leadership, a cool head, good old-fashioned 'common sense' and business nous are key ingredients. Those two years in France taught me a lot about the pressures of turning a company around, working in a different culture and dealing with militant unions. They also showed me the value of being transparent and visible, no matter how senior you are, and how essential it is to have mutual trust. The unions, the workers, the excellent management team – we couldn't have achieved what we did without trusting each other. And respecting one another, too.

Under the previous chairman, an autocrat who didn't allow people space to develop, the company had been floundering badly. Using a radical change in strategy, a focused, collaborative approach, and working overtly for the good of the company, we managed to turn it into a profitable enterprise with good long-term prospects. My next role would show me how strong leadership can sometimes hamper a company.

Meeting Mr Sugar

Turning companies around is a stressful business, but I knew I had an aptitude for it. The next two challenges I took on deepened my experience of different cultures and diverse ways of working, as well as providing further insight into how and why things go wrong – and how best to fix them.

Now that my 'adventure' in La Belle France was over, I was very pleased to be back home in London. I sent my CV to a number of head-hunters, and it didn't take too long before I was invited for an interview with Alexandra Workwear, a leading supplier of workwear uniforms. It transpired that they were looking for a chief executive to run their subsidiaries. You'll never guess where: France! And Spain was to be my base!

The good news was that I would be joining the main board of a quoted company. The bad news: I would once again be living away from home and away from my wife, children and family. I didn't like missing out on my children growing up, and all the family issues that that brings. Also,

I was concerned about how I would manage in Spain, as my Spanish was pretty basic.

At about the same time that I was negotiating the Alexandra Workwear job, a friend of a friend, Mark Simons, got in touch to say that his brother-in-law was looking for a senior person and had agreed to interview me. This was in 1991, and my meeting was with the formidable Mr Alan Sugar.

We met in an office on the third floor of Amstrad House – Amstrad's head office in Brentwood. Amstrad was the number-one supplier of home computers in Europe at the time, but what made the company so special was that when Alan Sugar founded it in 1968, he completely transformed the consumer electronics market with a series of 'blockbuster' products at prices that no competitor could come close to matching. He had a reputation for straight talking and not suffering fools.

We sat at a round desk, and Mr Sugar started to flick through my CV. I prepared myself for some tough questions. But none came. In fact, he said absolutely nothing. He just sat there glancing out, not appearing to look at me.

Bizarre, I thought. 'Um, shall I tell you a bit about myself, Mr Sugar?'

'Go on then.'

I launched into my spiel, telling him how brilliant I was, and what an asset I would be. As I was doing so, he was still idly turning the pages of my CV, but certainly not reading it. Occasionally he would mutter 'huh', which was pretty off-putting. After a while, I stopped talking, thinking that it was a complete waste of time. With that, Mr Sugar got up and walked out of the room, muttering something that sounded like 'Bored.' (It later transpired that he had said, 'I'll speak to my board.') I was flabbergasted and wondered how the interview had gone so badly wrong. Clearly, there was no job for me here, so I mentally prepared myself to move ahead with Alexandra Workwear.

I sat for a moment or two, readying to leave, when the group marketing director, Bernhard Steiner, charged into the room and exclaimed, 'Alan likes you! You've got the job!'

'Eh, what job?' I had absolutely no idea.

Bernhard sat down and explained. The job was to be European chairman and chief executive of Amstrad International, based in the outskirts of Paris. (It was as if I was cursed!) The salary was generous. It was a great deal and, even better, I saw it as a huge opportunity to be involved with Amstrad and, perhaps in time, with Alan Sugar.

I have never subsequently broached the subject of our initial encounter with Alan, but it is indelibly etched on my memory as a defining moment in my life.

I was to start immediately because the woman who had been running the French business, Marion Vannier, had suffered a nervous breakdown. She had been immensely successful at selling Amstrad products in the French market-place and was regarded as a superstar in France, having been named Businesswoman of the Year only a couple of years previously. Mme Vannier had built the Amstrad brand in France from the beginning, but now the business was on the wane and, since her departure, 'the wheels were coming off'. I was being parachuted in to try to sort things out. That appealed to me – by now, you know I like a challenge! It was exciting, certainly more so than Alexander Workwear would have been. It was too good an opportunity to pass up and, while it still involved being abroad, it would be much easier for me than being based in Spain.

I said yes to Amstrad and, on the following Monday, I arrived at their office in Paris. What greeted me was a company that was clearly in complete disarray.

Mme Vannier had been running everything in the company. Since no one else had been allowed to make any decisions – they were all merely 'yes men' – her departure was followed by chaos. You often find, when you are parachuted in to turn companies around, that a number of the key people have already left. In this case, it was the finance director, and no one else knew how to work the mainframe computer. This meant that we couldn't access the data to match up payments that had been made against outstanding invoices. Neither could we monitor our stock or orders properly. This left us with a poor visibility of our financial or trading position.

Most of the staff who remained had completely lost heart. Mme Vannier was not only the corporate memory, but seemed to have been the heart and soul of the business as well. Her footprints were all over the place and I couldn't hope to fill her shoes. Unlike my previous French experience, though, those of the senior team who *were* still there were pretty hopeless, with the exception of a few highly experienced salespeople. I managed to identify a small nucleus of people I thought I could trust and rely on, and started to work with them. In addition, there were some highly competent managers from Amstrad's UK head office who were holding the fort. In particular, I remember

Mike Ray, a senior accountant, as being very helpful, if not indispensable.

Still, the chaos was bewildering, and we were facing a constant stream of complaints from all quarters. The resellers were threatening to defect to other brands and the systems were not giving us pertinent information. We were firefighting on all fronts.

Amstrad had, in the past year, introduced a new range of computers – the 2000 series – which was intended to expand the company's reach from the home to the office and business markets. The problem was that they were suffering from inexplicable failure rates. The Amstrad engineers were working around the clock investigating the cause and had focused their attention on everything apart from the disk drives, because they were supplied by two huge, reputable US manufacturers (Western Digital and Seagate). But the length of time it was taking to get to the root of the matter was creating catastrophic problems with the resellers, who wanted to return their faulty stock and whose faith in the brand was becoming an issue.

The company was also facing increasing competition from the likes of Compaq, IBM and HP in the mass market. All in all, it was obvious that my role at Amstrad wasn't going to be easy!

After a week or so, having analysed the situation, I decided the best thing to do was to type up my thoughts, identifying the critical issues and highlighting the numerous problems, and fax them over to Mr Sugar. (Yes, in those days, fax machines were cutting edge!) I thought this was the right and professional thing to do, bearing in mind we had never actually properly spoken to each other and I hadn't seen him since my interview.

I began to send my list to the number I had identified as that of his private fax. Page one went through. Then, as I was sending the second page, the phone rang. It was him, and he was livid. Excepting the more colourful language, the message was: 'I am not paying you all this money for you to tell me what the problems are. Don't speak to me again until you have fixed it.' And the phone went dead.

Although this second encounter with Mr Sugar was even worse than the first, on the upside, he had finally spoken to me! Furthermore, while I had imagined I was doing the right thing by keeping him informed, I now knew he didn't want to hear about the issues; what he wanted from me was just to get on with it. Great. Music to my ears. Sort of.

In the early days Mr Sugar had had a few senior people coming over periodically from head office to help sort out the mess, so in reality he had a pretty good handle on what was going on. But I now owned the problem, and was left to my own devices to sort things out and turn the company around. That suited me fine.

The first thing I did was to set about trying to reassure the company's network of resellers that we would fix the product issue. At the same time, I needed to work with the sales team to explain how we were going to get through this with a workaround – usually by offering generous discounts to keep the resellers on board – and ensure that they knew what to tell those resellers about the faulty product. I recruited an excellent finance director, Anthony Komedera, who worked tirelessly with the UK team to get the systems up and running.

Slowly but surely, the business stabilised. New computers with faster processors and colour screens (the 386 and 486) were coming on stream and we replaced the faulty old models, offering advantageous terms for resellers taking on the new ranges. Now most of our time was spent keeping the resellers on board, and trying to encourage those who had defected to other brands to come back to Amstrad. It was clear, however, that the competition had not stood idly by while our problems were being addressed.

Twelve months had passed and I still hadn't heard another thing from the boss. Then, one day, quite out of the blue, I got a call from Mr Sugar, announcing that he was coming to Paris and I was to meet him at the airport.

As instructed, I went to pick him up. I felt nervous. Many stories had filtered through about the man, and, as I had had first-hand experience, I felt unsettled. The one reassuring thing I had heard, from his brother-in-law, was that not hearing from Alan was the most positive indication – it meant he had confidence in you. If he was on the phone and looking over your shoulder all the time, that's when there was likely to be trouble. And now, here he was, in Paris.

Having collected Alan from the airport, I was driving him back to the office when I missed the turning off the Peripherique. Annoyed with myself, I was just about to swear, when I suddenly thought, No, I had better not. Must act professional. So, instead of exclaiming, 'Oh shit, I've missed the exit,' I came out with: 'Oh sugar!' Oh dear.

At the office, Mr Sugar assembled my team in the board-room. Once the motley crew were in place, he pointed randomly at one of the petrified sales managers, and then at me, and said, 'Is he any good?' Now, this sales manager did not speak one word of English, and Alan does not speak

French, so, unsure of what he was being asked, the sales manager just said, '*Non.*'

I am sure that, for the first time, I noticed a glimmer of a smile on Alan's face. He understood the confusion. Turning to me, he said, 'Right, Claude, I am going to leave the room for a few minutes. Talk to your people and when I come back they had all better give me the right answer.'

I explained to my team in simple terms: 'Look, he doesn't speak French, so if he asks you a question, please just say "*oui*".'

Alan walked back in and, pointing to one of the lame ducks and then to me, said, 'He's rubbish, isn't he?

'*Oui*,' came the pitiful reply.

And with that, I took Mr Sugar back to the airport.

The following day, I got a call from the boss: 'Claude, come back to London, you are finished there.'

I protested, 'I think you may have got the wrong impression yesterday. I am doing a good job here, and there is still more to do, but we are on the right track.'

'Claude, I'm not interested in all that. Your work's done there. Be back in London tomorrow. And come to see me.'

I was devastated but what could I do? The next day I was in London, in his office, again trying to explain that I really was doing a good job, but that it was a big situation to turn around and would take time. He said, 'Claude, I know you are doing a good job. That's why I have asked you to come back. I need you to do the same thing in Spain. We have real problems there. If you think France is bad, wait 'til you see what is happening over there.'

I had heard via the grapevine that Amstrad Spain was in big, big trouble. On the one hand, I was relieved that I was not being fired, but on the other, I was a bit sceptical about going to Spain and facing yet another stint away from my family. I agreed to take it, on the condition that it had to be the last job I did abroad, and that when I got back I'd be appointed to the main board of Amstrad. That was agreed, on the proviso that I did a good job.

*

Amstrad France had been a baptism of fire. The company had been in freefall after a failing product line and the sad departure of its inspirational chief executive. I had managed, with a lot of help from the UK and certain key French employees, to put the fire out and get the company back on its feet. But if France had been a baptism of fire, Spain was nearly a cremation.

Siesta and fiesta

In 1992, I arrived at the head office of Amstrad España, at a place called Tres Cantos, on the outskirts of Madrid. Unlike Amstrad's head office in Paris, which consisted of a large, shed-like warehouse with fairly utilitarian offices above, this was a stunning, ultra-modern, white office building adorned with artwork and expensive furnishings and a massive, new, beautifully racked out warehouse adjoining it.

I called the team together to explain what was happening. I had to speak in Spanish, which was tricky for me; it was effectively my third language, which I'd learned at school, so it was really not good at all. However, whereas I had once fretted over the correct French for 'You're fired' before arriving at Les Trois Lords – because I am bilingual in French – I was conversely quite happy to use incorrect tenses, or words that may not have actually existed, when trying to speak Spanish. I just ploughed my way through what I wanted to say and left it at that.

However, I had recently done my back in and was

hobbling somewhat, so as I finished my talk and left the open-plan office I was bent over, clutching my back like an old cartoon crone. As I exited, I glanced back to see a bunch of them mimicking me, taking the piss. Not a good start for me . . . or for them!

Sometimes people think that I am overly interfering and aggressive, but I think that comes from a genuine curiosity to understand things from the ground up. I really am interested in every cog and wheel in a business, so I want to find out as much as I can, then get involved and think of better ways of doing things.

At Amstrad Spain, I decided not to move into the palatial, corner-office suite my predecessor had occupied, with its huge mahogany desk, leather sofas and expensive fixtures and fittings. Instead, I set myself up in a small office with clear glass, just off the open-plan office area, so I could keep an eye on what was going on. I wanted to be an integral part of the action. But at Amstrad España, there really wasn't any!

On my first day there, after I had made my call to action, I worked away in my unassuming office, poring over reports and figures, completely absorbed in what I was doing for a couple of hours. I looked up to give myself a break, only to discover that everyone had disappeared. There wasn't a soul left in the office.

Shit. What had I said? Had my impassioned plea to pull together and turn this thing around been misinterpreted. Had I mangled my message? Well, one thing was for sure – I was not going to send a fax to Mr Sugar! I had a better idea. I would man up. I phoned him to let him know that I may have a problem, as all the staff had walked out.

'Don't be daft', he said. 'It's lunchtime! They will be having their siesta! They'll be back.' And sure enough, at 4.00 p.m. they all reappeared and stayed 'working' until 8.00 p.m. That was how it operated there. No one had bothered to tell me!

I was very fortunate in Amstrad Spain in that I inherited two helpful and knowledgeable young managers: Violetta, our in-house lawyer, and an accountant, Rafa. They both smoked like chimneys, but they were a godsend. They spoke good English and, with Violetta's knowledge of Spanish law and Rafa's skill with the numbers, I was sure that, with their support, I could make the turnaround work.

As in France, the Spanish subsidiary had suffered from the 2000 series computer fiasco, but the market in Spain was somewhat different: a good proportion of the business was in set-top boxes, satellite dishes and other consumer electronic products. The problems within the Spanish company were somewhat different as well. Mme Vannier had at least left a well-staffed company capable of functioning at a professional level, once we'd fixed some of the problems. In Spain, there was no solid infrastructure and the staff, by and large, were pretty useless – lacking any motivation or discipline. The whole atmosphere was of a company in terminal decline. It was clear that the immediate task was to try to breathe new life into a failing business.

The staff were a problem. For example, we had an AS400 mainframe computer system, which I could see from my office. One employee, called Javier, spent all day long walking back and forth in front of the air-conditioned room in which the mainframe was located. What is that all about? I wondered. Eventually, I couldn't stand it any more.

I asked him, 'What is your job?'

'I thinking.'

'What about?'

'Just thinking.'

'So what else do you do?' It turned out that he switched on the AS400 in the morning and off again at night – and probably also did a bit of monitoring and backing up of data – but that was it.

'I'm sorry,' I told him, 'you are going to have to contribute a bit more than that.'

After that he did try to look busier, and at least stopped walking up and down the corridor all day, but I don't think he was really doing very much. Then, a month later, I noticed someone I had never seen before talking to Javier, and asked Violetta who he was. It turned out that he was the mainframe thinker's boss, the IT director – a man I had never previously seen in the building. He only came in once a month.

I popped into Rafa's office and checked the payroll. The IT director was earning a very good salary for dropping in on a monthly basis. I came back out of Rafa's office, and sacked them both.

In Amstrad España, there was no problem with invoicing customers, or having accurate management information to hand. The invoices went out and were properly recorded, but, critically, no one was chasing the overdue accounts, and, rather than getting to the root of the query, credit notes were being issued as a way of resolving problems. Customers would order products, but no one was checking to see if their accounts were overdue, or if their cheques had bounced. Returns were being accepted from retailers by the third-party warehouse without being properly authorised.

The managing director, Juan, was a charming man, but entered into uncommercial transactions, was out of touch with what was going on, and tended to fall back on '*mañana*' and half-truths when I would challenge him on calling customers and getting them to pay up. I made compromise agreements with Juan and Ignacio, the finance director, both of whom had presided over the mess I had inherited.

I could see from the aged debtor reports that Amstrad Spain was owed a lot of money, so I reorganised the office, and made it an absolute priority for everyone to focus on collecting overdue accounts. Many customers had small invoice issues, but were unwilling to settle any part of the debt unless their queries were dealt with. We were very hard on customers who still failed to pay once we had sent them copy invoices, or proof of delivery on the items they claimed to have never received.

With Rafa and Violetta working in tandem, if customers failed to pay after we had resolved their issues, Violetta issued a seven-day letter, and, without further recourse, froze the account and instructed debt recovery lawyers to begin legal action. These initiatives proved highly successful and the weekly list analysing overdue accounts began to shrink considerably until the company bank balance looked healthier. Unfortunately, a number of customers had been allowed too much credit and, when we chased them for payment, turned out to have no means of settling.

There were other nonsensical practices. For example, broken models of a line of Amstrad products – computer-gaming joysticks, pistols and the like – were returned for repairs. This was undertaken by a firm of subcontractors in a warehouse in which Amstrad rented space. There, on a mezzanine floor, was an army of people repairing, recon-ditioning and then reboxing these inexpensive products. Once repaired, they were sent out to retailers, at which point they often failed again and were returned once more to be fixed. Each repair cost £30, but the product only cost £15 in the first place! I stopped this process at once: not another repair. It was better to take the loss and throw the stuff away than try to repair such a low-value and trouble-some product.

Perhaps the most galling example of skulduggery was per-petrated by the Amstrad agency in Tenerife, who serviced the Canary Islands from their base. They owed Amstrad Spain a lot of money for products we had shipped to them. It was always '*mañana*' when we asked for payment. I decided to fly over and meet with the principals, with a view to collecting payment. They had a small warehouse piled high with boxes of Amstrad products. That was a relief, I thought; even if I couldn't retrieve the money owed, at least I could reclaim the stock. I said to them, 'Listen, you have all this stock. Why aren't you paying us?' Yet another reassurance came that they would, but something wasn't right. So I gently kicked a few of the boxes. They had a hollow sound, as if they were perhaps empty.

I decided to take a look at the stock and asked them to open some of the boxes. Empty! I started to pick up other boxes. They were also empty. Occasionally I came across a box with something in it. When I opened it I found junk, old parts, rubbish.

I was livid. 'I want the money you owe us. I don't care about your stock.' I told them I would not leave until I had a cheque for the money they owed. Eventually they agreed and I left with the cheque, in the form of a *pagare*, a promissory note.

I was very pleased with myself, and the following morning I presented the note to Rafa to deposit in the bank. A few days later, it bounced. I flew back to Tenerife in a rage, but they were gone! Nothing there at all. They had vanished completely and I never saw or heard from them again.

These were just a few examples of how things in the company had been allowed to slip out of hand. No one had been looking at anything rigorously enough; there was turmoil and a sense of drift everywhere. It just shows how easy it is to do. When you're in business, and particularly when you're in charge, you have to be relentless in making sure that bad practice, wasteful habits and don't-care attitudes don't creep in and get established, like some spreading garden weed.

Sacking lazy and useless employees and stopping the pointless loss-making repairs had a very beneficial effect on morale and the attitude within the company. People seemed to start to take things more seriously – working late and trying different things to make the company successful.

While I was fixing waste and uncommercial practices within the company, the negotiations with the major supermarkets and retail stockists of Amstrad products were proving more difficult. Eventually I reached an amicable arrangement with three supermarket groups, Continente, Pryca and Alcampo. They had strong demand for Amstrad products, in particular our satellite products, and I agreed to relieve them of slow-moving products, thereby clearing the way for the business relationship to move forward.

However, with El Corte Ingles, a major department store in Spain (their version of the UK's John Lewis), I came to a complete impasse over the return of stock. They wanted to return it all; I wanted them to pay for the sellable stock and then talk about the refunds. At one meeting my frustration boiled over and I gave them a menacing glare and told them in no uncertain terms what they could do with their proposal. I was speaking in English because my Spanish was nowhere near good enough to convey my sentiments. Violetta, however, calmly translated: 'Mr Littner was wondering if you would be so kind as to perhaps reconsider your position on this matter.' Just as well, as I would most likely have been removed by Security if her translation had been verbatim. I am absolutely single-minded when I throw myself into the rescue mission – using every ounce of energy I can gather and unleashing my venom on anyone who gets in the way! I am a lot calmer now for reasons that will become apparent.

Even given all these problems, the company was doing some business and the mistakes of the past were being addressed and resolved. I had been in Amstrad Spain for some months when I received a phone call from Alan. 'I want you to try and sell the head office building and warehouse, and close the business.'

'But we are getting somewhere here,' I pleaded.

'I understand that, and you are doing a great job, but it is simply impossible to make a go of that business. What you need to do is to continue to collect overdue accounts, but, at the same time, do what needs to be done to close the company down. The strategy going forward will be for Amstrad plc to support its products in the Spanish market through an independent distributor.'

I wrote Alan a comprehensive report outlining all the reasons why I thought it would be advisable to keep the Spanish subsidiary going. I ended by stating: 'I don't know the big picture, so I hope you will understand that my motives are guided by what I believe to be in the best interests of Amstrad. In any event, you can count on me one hundred per cent to complete my responsibilities in Spain to the best of my ability.'

I explained the situation to Violetta and Rafa. They accepted the decision, and we set about changing tack. Over the next few months, I reduced the workforce, so that we ended up with just Rafa, Violetta and me. Rafa and Violetta were excellent throughout and were well rewarded for their hard work and loyalty. Indeed, Violetta moved to a law firm and became the Amstrad representative in Spain, tying up the loose ends.

I came to an agreement with a service repair centre called MADE in Barcelona to take on the legal commitment for all Amstrad's in- and out-of-warranty products. I have dismissed this deal in a single sentence, but in fact it was not an easy negotiation to complete. All manufacturers are obliged to repair or replace in-warranty products, and retain spare parts in order to service all out-of-warranty products for a period of five years. So concluding this deal was an essential precondition of Amstrad's exit from Spain.

Alan had had serious doubts that it would be possible to actually sell the head office and warehouse, in spite of the fact that it was a magnificent place. In his view, never mind the white building, it was a white elephant – in the wrong location. Against the odds, I was able to negotiate an excellent price for this white elephant. Finally, I had done something to please Alan!

*

And that was it for me. My European adventures, I thought, had at last come to an end, and I was looking forward to finally securing a well-deserved position back in the UK as a main board director of Amstrad plc.

'It's like World War Three in there!'

When I was seventeen, one of my friends announced that he intended to become a psychiatrist. Sure enough, that's what he is today. However, I don't think that many people get to plan their careers out that precisely. Certainly, in my case, since attaining my first degree in 1972, I had been involved in the chemicals and meat business, retail, aircraft servicing, plumbing, management consultancy, shirt manufacturing and consumer electronics.

I had started and run a successful business, turned some companies around and witnessed others sunk by incompetence or an inability to let go and move on. But if someone had suggested, when the teacher had first consigned me to *fond de la classe*, that by now I'd have seen so much, and been able to test my abilities in such diverse businesses, I think anyone who knew me then would have laughed and quickly changed the subject.

Having said that, if I had been asked to evaluate my CV by this point, I would have had to scratch my head and wonder where this bloke was going. He's all over the place! And now I was about to make a switch from one kind of business to a whole other ball game – literally.

Both Amstrad France and Spain had been highly successful, but by the time I became involved they were well past their heyday. However, I had brought order to the total chaos that had confronted me on my arrival, and did my utmost to restore confidence and extract value. So I returned to London with an understanding that I had a home-based job and a seat on the main Amstrad board waiting for me. Things, as usual, did not prove to be that straightforward.

When I strode into Amstrad's head office back in London, the person I was meant to be taking over from was still sitting in what I had thought would be my office. I immediately spoke to Alan.

'Do you know he's still here?'

'I know, Claude, but he's been here from the beginning and I just can't let him go. You can have any other job in the company, pretty much, but not his. In fact, I have another fantastic opportunity, which I think will be perfect for you. I have bought it out of receivership. Cutting-edge stuff. It's a mobile phone manufacturer that went bust. So I want you to go in, employ the staff you need and get the company up and running again . . .'

'Where is this company?'

'Aalborg.'

'Al who?'

'Aalborg, Denmark.'

'Alan, my wife will kill me. I promised her Spain would be my very last job abroad.'

'Claude, do this for me. Just for a few months and I promise you I will bring you back. I need you to get things underway there.'

Working in Paris was a hop, skip and a jump to get back to London at weekends. Madrid was a bit of a jump. Upper Jutland, where Dancall, the company in question, was located, was a bloody long way with a change of planes at Copenhagen!

Anyway, I went to Dancall Radio – a Danish cordless and mobile telephone company – in August 1993, and found that Amstrad had acquired very modern, up-to-date offices and research facilities, a fully functioning state-of-the-art factory, the Dancall brand and the intellectual property rights in various Dancall products. The purchase price was £6.4 million.

'200 jobs at Amstrad'.

However, I also found that I was the only employee. Imagine walking into a huge modern factory with a superbly kitted-out office block on site – with no one there. Not a soul. That's what it was like when I arrived at Dancall. A bit spooky. At that moment, I realised the magnitude of the task that Alan had set me. Fortunately, the receiver put me in contact with the previous managing director's PA, who, he assured me, was excellent. Having recruited her, I was able to quickly make contact with a number of the key members of the management team and employ them to help me get the company up and running. Within a very short space of time, I had taken on two hundred Dancall employees, laid off when the company went into suspension of payments, all of whom were very pleased indeed to be back at work and keen and committed to restoring the fortunes of Dancall.

It seemed to me that once again Alan had pulled off a coup. Dancall had been a leader in European mobile tele-communications technology and sold cellular and cordless telephones in more than twenty-five countries worldwide. It was one of the last established European stand-alone mobile equipment businesses still to design, assemble and market its own branded range of products. It had the potential to get back on its feet and be successful.

But I had carried over my modus operandi from my time working in Spain, where, apart from Violetta and Rafa, the staff had only been interested in siesta and fiesta – always promising to get things done 'mañana'. My mindset for countering this behaviour was deeply ingrained and I carried it with me to Denmark.

After a week or so, my new PA asked me if I had some

form of 'mental problem'. 'What are you talking about?' I barked at her.

'Well, you are going around shouting at everyone. Honestly, if you want something done, just ask, and we will do it.'

I had a reality check. I reminded myself that I was now working with gentle, professional and diligent people. I did have a bit of a déjà vu moment, though, on the day I popped into the newly re-established Research and Development Department and found a group of pipe-smoking engineers in woolly jumpers just walking around, deep in thought. Oh no, not another lot of 'Javiers', I thought. Here, though, that was not the case. They were working, under instruction from Alan, on developing more advanced versions of DECT technology for a new range of digital cordless phones, to complement the range of cellular phones.

Even in those first few weeks we created a proper, functioning operation. The Research and Development Department was working effectively, and the previously empty factory was actually turning out mobile phones, for which we had advance orders. Indeed, I had it in mind that when the first cellular phone came off the production line, I'd send it to Alan; but in the end I thought he would rather have had the sale! When I look at the unbelievable power and minute size of today's mobile phones, what were considered highly desirable cellular phones in the early nineties seem like heavy brick-like devices with limited battery life and usability. That's technology for you!

Almost before I knew it, Bob Watkins, Amstrad's long-serving technical director, was despatched to take over from

me, and I was on my way home. Incidentally, Amstrad sold
Dancall to Bosch Telecom in 1997 for £90 million – quite
a nice return on the original £6.4 million investment.

Back in London again, Alan called me into his office. 'I've
got one more job for you, Claude, right here in London . . .
You are going to Spurs.'

'Spurs? No I'm not.'

'Claude, you've got to. It's like World War Three in there.
There are problems everywhere. You're the only one who
can sort it out. It's perfect for you. You'll love it!'

'But Alan, I've worked very hard to get into the mainstream Amstrad business. You told me that was what my
next move would be, and now you are saying I am to go to
Spurs. That's not what I want.'

Of course, on reflection, Alan had provided me with
the opportunity of great business experience and honing
my skills in France, Spain and Denmark, and now he was
inviting me to take up yet another challenge. It would have
been madness to refuse.

I joined Tottenham Hotspur Football Club as CEO in
November 1993. I arrived at a time when the club was in
total turmoil. The place was, indeed, the business equivalent
of Armageddon. But I didn't let my lifelong attachment to
the club get in the way of my decisions and approach to
working there. Far from it: I was more determined than
ever to make it successful.

Earlier, in May 1993, Alan, in his capacity as chairman,
had sacked Terry Venables, the chief executive, who was
responsible for running the football side of things. Terry
was a former Tottenham and England player and had managed both Crystal Palace and Queens Park Rangers before

Sugar brings on his new man for Spurs

TOTTENHAM HOTSPUR yesterday named the man to replace Terry Venables. He is 44-year-old Claude Littner, one of Spurs' chairman Alan Sugar's chief business lieutenants.

As managing director, Littner will head the football club's commercial operations. But, unlike Venables whose title was chief executive, he will not have any involvement with the team.

Sacked

Sugar yesterday described Littner as someone with a "mainstream business background".

The appointment fills the position left vacant when Terry Venables was sacked by Sugar in May, triggering a legal battle which it was revealed yesterday has cost the club £550,000.

Ossie Ardiles, the new manager appointed in

By ANDREW MOODY

June, has already taken over Venables' football responsibilities.

Littner, an ex-Unilever executive who for the past two years has headed the overseas operations of Sugar's **Amstrad** business, will mastermind Spurs' multi-million pound commercial business.

Yesterday, the club announced a 10 per cent rise in profits in the year to May from £3.06 million to £3.36 million.

Apart from the court costs with Venables, £600,000 of repairs to the East Stand also dented profits.

If star players Paul Gascoigne and Paul Stewart had not been sold, the club would have been almost in the red. They brought in receipts totalling £3.23 million.

A factual newspaper article announcing my arrival at Spurs. The press were less gentle about me in future articles.

arriving at Tottenham in 1987. Things were getting nasty and Alan's attention was focused on the courtroom saga that was going on to determine if he indeed had the right to dismiss Venables. Of course, he did!

However, at Spurs there were so many warring factions and splits just at a time when harmony was needed. Remember, in addition to the internal turmoil in the club, the newly formed Premier League was still finding its feet and there were many issues relating to that. The case of Terry Venables was another point of disagreement. There were those fans and media commentators who were supporters of Irving Scholar (the previous chairman and lifelong Spurs fan). Others strongly favoured Venables, who was being portrayed as the local hero. Yet others were supporters of Ossie Ardiles, who had been appointed first team manager. However, the one who had put his money in to rescue the club turned out to be the least favoured of all. There's nowt as strange as folk.

In the first chapter of this book, I described my first day at Spurs and just one of the multitude of problems, big and small, that confronted me. Performance on the pitch was suffering from the turmoil occurring off the pitch. Meanwhile, football as a whole was just beginning to wake up to the financial implications of the huge television rights deal that the Premier League had landed with Sky.

In 1992, the TV rights for the Premier League had been sold to Sky for £191 million, a figure that would later soar. It is now over £5 billion per season. Even in those early days, though, the impact on each club (and players' demands) was huge and there was inevitably a difference of opinion between the playing staff and the business about how the money could best be used. But to be honest, everywhere you looked, money was leaking. In addition to the numerous problems you might find in many companies, at Tottenham there were three very significant additional dimensions.

The first point to consider was that *everyone* involved, either directly or indirectly, with the club was a stakeholder. The board, fans, sponsors, players, administrative staff, manager, local council and residents near the ground – everyone felt that they owned the club and that their views and ideas were right and should be implemented straight away. Not only that, of course, but every other week – at the home matches – 36,000 people got to vent their frustration and anger directly at you! (Not to mention the public scrutiny through the televised games.) The perpetual clamour for change and demands for improvements were the soundtrack to my time as CEO.

The second dimension to this role was that everything I did (and I mean *everything*) appeared in the press – usually with only a distant relationship to the truth, and always with a negative spin. If the business problems were reasonably familiar, the scale, visibility and resultant public profile were new and not very welcome. I've never courted publicity or wanted to be in the public eye – I like fixing things from the inside, not being the 'face' of a business.

The third element of the job involved trying to reconcile two competing faces of Tottenham: Tottenham Hotspur Football and Athletics Company – a football club with intense, loyal, committed fans who only wanted success on the pitch, at whatever price – and Tottenham Hotspur plc, the business. The latter was a fully listed company on the London Stock Exchange, and the demands of the Regulatory Authority are stringent. For example, financially sensitive information needs to be provided in a timely fashion to the market. A public company needs to show a stable financial performance, as well as a clear dividend policy for shareholders.

Tottenham was always a club first and a business second – a strange hybrid that the financial analysts questioned at the time. Getting the two aspects of the club happily to share the same bed was a real challenge.

During that first week, while I was again working into the early evening, I looked out of my window down to the car park and saw it was still full of cars – staff cars, as this wasn't a match day. I thought to myself, That's good. If these people are still working at 6.30 p.m., then it's going to be all right. There's passion and dedication being shown here which we can use.' I was pleased.

At 7.30 p.m., the car park was still pretty full. No bad thing, I thought. These people care. If there is a strong nucleus of good people working here, I can harness that to sort out the problems. Excellent.

I left at around 8.30 p.m. or so, and was walking down from my third-floor office when I heard the sound of laughter from the first-floor box-holders' area, which is where some of the hospitality lounges are located. Very good, I thought, we have a function on, bringing in cash.

I popped my head in just to have a quick look, and saw it was full of our staff, having a right old meet-up with friends. And the bar was very much open – handing over free drinks to whoever held out a hand.

I went over to Peter Barnes, the club secretary, to ask what the hell was going on. 'We often get together. You have to understand, Claude: this is a club; it isn't just any other business.'

'It may be a club to the players, Peter, and the fans and sponsors, but it isn't a club for you. This is a job! Those shutters are coming down right now and this is not going to happen again. When you finish work you leave – go home, to your family or wherever you want – but not to sit here and have drinks on the house.'

I marched out very clear in my mind that I had mended another leaky tap. But in this instance, I had neglected to understand what Peter had told me: it was a club before it was a business. League results mattered more than financial ones.

*

In this chapter I want to give you some examples of things that were happening off the field. Tottenham's performance on the field is well documented and I won't add anything of significance there, but I think it is interesting to reveal the issues that people in football administration have to deal with, and the complex and sometimes strange problems that are part of the normal working day.

The first strategic review I presented to the board in June 1994, after seven months in the job, gives a sense of the breadth of my responsibilities. In this note, I covered the following areas:

Admin and accounts	Season tickets
Legal	Salaries
Property	Match day staff
Training ground	Coaching Department
Warehouse	Travel
Office moves	Catering
West Stand improvements	Press and PR
South Stand	Pensions
Sponsorship	Physio/medical Department
Ticket office	Insurance
Parking facilities	Stadium use (by third parties)
Match day privileges	Memorabilia
Corporate hospitality	External contacts

There was quite a lot to get stuck into!

I set about my work, though, in the same way that I had everywhere else: analysing every contract, scrutinising every line in the management accounts, stamping out any silly spending as soon as I saw it, and monitoring every invoice that came in and every cheque that went out. I asked questions about everything. Sometimes I got this right and sometimes I got it wrong – I once naively asked why the Premier League didn't allocate local officials – referees and linesmen – to the matches so that we could save on their travel expenses! The suggestion was absurd from a football-ing perspective, but shows that I was considering every cost imaginable. The press had a field day with that one.

I tried to fix things at my normal speed, but change is not something that comes easily in football. Back then, it was all steeped in tradition and had a rather old-fashioned way of doing business. It soon became clear that it was going to be very difficult to change anything, because the football fraternity (including football journalists, who always know best!) is a closed shop – and I was seen as an outsider. From day one, reports appeared in the press about my 'brutal' cost-cutting measures.

The way these stories were reported was scandalous. Just two months after I had taken up my role, a report appeared in one of the tabloids under the headline 'Sugar's Bitter Pal Row'. In it, the charges against me were repeated at great length, one of which was that my cash-saving measures included 'cutting back on food at the training ground'. This was absolute nonsense and purely mischievous. In fact, what had happened was that I had observed the players eating massive (and I mean huge) fry-ups every day after their morning training and had advocated that they have healthy, nutritious food instead! Something, by the way, that is fully recognised and absolutely adhered to now.

There was all sorts of nonsense. One tabloid alleged that I had stopped Gary Mabbutt, the hugely respected and much-loved club captain, who was diabetic, from having his regular supply of Coca-Cola. It was utter rubbish, but it all got printed, with me cast as the pantomime villain.

Hospitality was another area in which there were all kinds of problems. The profile of Spurs was such that we attracted a lot of companies to entertain clients there. We had boxes for corporate hospitality, which companies would buy for a season or multiple seasons, and these proved an excellent revenue source for the club and served as a wonderful venue for corporate entertainment.

However, as I was going through the numbers, I noticed what appeared to be a discrepancy. Quite a few of the owners of corporate hospitality boxes hadn't paid a penny. I asked our commercial manager, Mike Rollo, about it.

'They never pay.'

'Well then, don't let them in!'

'You can't do that, Claude.'

In years gone by, these companies had done the club a good turn and we had paid them back with a box for a couple of seasons, but twenty years later, the deal was still continuing. It was like a grace-and-favour arrangement. No one had ever challenged the situation.

'I don't think that's fair,' I said. 'They have to pay. Next week is the Manchester United game, and I want you to call each of these companies and tell them that if they don't pay the full rate for the box, they can't use it.'

'They will go apeshit.'

'I don't care. They have to pay if they want a box.'

Others weren't scheduled to pay until the end of that season. I wasn't having that either. I needed the cashflow, so I put a stop to that practice as well. And of course the companies paid. They kicked and screamed, and probably hated me, but they had enjoyed a nice run for their money – and it was now over.

Quite early on in my time there, I remember looking around at one game and reflecting happily that we had another full house – 36,000 fans filling the seats. On the Monday I popped into the ticket office to confirm that we had indeed had a full house. I checked the receipts with the in-house accountant and just could not understand why the cash takings came up short.

I looked into it and, after further investigation, the source of the discrepancies became very clear. Suffice it to say that there were a number of pretty dodgy practices that had been going on for years. The following season I implemented a ticket-only entry system and did away with cash turnstiles, as well as rectifying a number of other issues. I think Spurs were the first club to initiate 'all-ticket' matches.

Wherever I looked in those early days, it felt like people were taking advantage of the club. Tottenham was like a rich relative who just provided them with whatever they needed. Perhaps I went in too hard in challenging the culture at the outset, but I felt it had to be done, and, I think, in the end we led the way in the Premier League as far as getting costs under control was concerned.

Amidst all this chaos, with money and stories leaking all

over the place, we did professionalise the running of the club. Alan Sugar chaired all the monthly board meetings, we had accurate and informative management accounts, we analysed and scrutinised the information, and we had a plan to work to. This gave us a clear handle on our incomings and outgoings, and what we could invest in new players and other projects. Of course, being football, the budgets were often thrown off course. On more than one occasion Alan would compliment me on achieving a good piece of incremental business, then, almost in the same breath, inform me that all that hard work had just evaporated with the securing of a new player's contract.

Perhaps the outside world didn't see it, but the club was under much better control. It was becoming a proper business. We plugged a lot of the holes and managed to build two new stands – at the north and south ends of the stadium – on time and on budget (unlike Wembley and some other Premier League redevelopments). Alan was particularly proud of the huge Jumbotron screen he had insisted upon as part of the new north and south stand redevelopment. These are now commonplace at Premier League stadiums, but we led the way. He also derived pleasure from now being able to walk through the whole stadium, as all parts were now connected.

Of course, the new stands were not down to me: the architect, Igal Yawetz, masterminded the project, but I made sure that Mowlem, the builders, kept to schedule and budget. I spent time every day with the excellent property manager, Simon Wood, and his right-hand man, Jim Hughes, walking round the building site, making sure things were as specified and making adjustments where necessary.

It wasn't just the structures that needed looking after; the council and the local residents had to be satisfied and pacified. There were many facets to the projects – and a number of things going on behind the scenes of which the fans were blissfully unaware. We had been asked to resurrect a closed Tube station very close to the ground, fund a new library, install new streetlights, buy up local properties – the list seemed endless!

My relationship with the fans was always testy, although Alan took the brunt of the abuse. I got a bit of a reputation over time for being a bit too forthright in my appraisal of their insights. Several of my choice responses to fans' letters were sent to the press, or ended up in the Spurs fanzine, *Cock-a-Doodle-Doo*, under the heading 'Dear Alan, Dear Claude'.

One of my letters in particular prompted a headline in the *Daily Mirror* that asked: 'Is This the Rudest Man in Football?' It came about because I had responded to a fan's comments about our injury crisis. The comments alleged a lack of competence and professionalism in the way we looked after the players. My ill-advised reply is worth quoting in full:

> *Your comments regarding the injury situation display a high level of ignorance and downright stupidity. We take every care and precaution with all our players. Referrals are always made to the leading specialists and second opinions regularly sought in order to ensure that the right medical decisions and follow-up treatment are effected. Newspapers make ridiculous statements and comments and some gullible fans such as yourself just believe the garbage.*
>
> *Thank you for writing and sharing your concerns.*

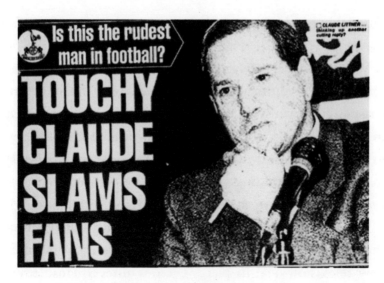

A letter to a fan unsurprisingly found its way into
the newspapers with a typically unsympathetic slant.

Culture is very important. I had understood that at the
shirt company in France, and had it pointed out to me in
Denmark, but here, somehow, I didn't quite get it right.

I did get a grip on all the business issues though. I recognised early on that merchandise was a potentially very
lucrative revenue stream. Unfortunately, the club shops were
pokey little stores on Tottenham High Street, which generated very little money, since they couldn't accommodate
the smallest fraction of the average home crowd. We also,
from some strange legacy, had shops in Birmingham and
Leicester that were losing money hand over fist. Meanwhile,
there was a warehouse overflowing with replica shirts, mugs
and so on.

With my retail experience, and through observing what
'the mob down the road' (Arsenal – for you non-football
fans) was doing, it was obvious that we needed to create a

superstore on the high road alongside the stadium to satisfy the huge demand.

We built one superstore, extended another and created a space in the stadium where merchandise could also be purchased. Turnover went through the roof – a tenfold increase in revenue – and the stores were rammed with fans eager to purchase our new and extensive range of Spurs branded merchandise (including mail order). This became a very nice profit centre within the club.

Of course, there were also new club and shirt sponsorship agreements to negotiate, and with the highly lucrative new television deal in place, these contracts became very significant. I was very fortunate to have Alan's son, Daniel Sugar, in the Marketing Department, and he became a close confidant and an outstanding negotiator – a real chip off the old block.

During one close season, Daniel negotiated a first-team tour of the Far East, with exhibition matches in Hong Kong and China. This was highly lucrative, and Daniel and I went to the Far East together to close the deal and seek out further sponsorship opportunities. I have never enjoyed a business trip so much.

I was always looking to generate more revenue for the club. One year, I entered into a contract with the London Monarchs, who paid the club one million pounds to play American football at White Hart Lane towards the end of our season – just half a dozen games or so. It was good business because it made use of the ground when Spurs were playing away, and there was a revenue share over and above the contracted amount.

The downside was that they messed up the pitch. During the last home game of our season, just as Teddy Sheringham was about to score, the ball bobbled up and he missed a sitter. Whether that imperfection on the pitch was caused by the American football games is impossible to say. Teddy certainly thought so. After the game, when Alan and I were down in the dressing room talking to the manager and players, he came up to us and insisted he would have scored if it hadn't been for that '******* American football and that ******* awful pitch'.

We had already decided that we were going to lay a new pitch during the close season. Indeed, that is why I had agreed to the American football matches. Our pitch, even without those matches, wasn't good enough – not when compared to Arsenal's. Yes, we had under-soil heating and all that, but the turf, and the earth beneath, had become so compacted that the drainage wasn't as effective as it needed to be, or as befitted a Premier League club. Doing all the work on the pitch and substructure was a significant expense, so I thought getting a chunk of money in to help pay for it was a smart move.

Immediately after the last match of the season, the diggers came in and removed the 'hallowed' turf, all the compacted earth and the under-soil heating. The schedule of work was quite specific and intense; no delays could be entertained and everything had to be ship shape for the first game of the new season – less than three months away. The new turf itself had been purchased many months before and was being lovingly cultivated and tended by groundsmen in the Sheffield area.

We were doing well and were on track. Then Chelsea Football Club, who were also renovating their pitch at

Stamford Bridge, approached me and offered quite a large sum of money to buy the turf from us. My initial reaction: obviously not, that would be plain crazy! But then I thought about it and reckoned that kind of money doesn't grow on trees!

I had a chat with our head groundsman and asked if there was any alternative to laying down the turf we had bought. He couldn't fathom why we would need to consider an alternative when we had gone to all the trouble to have turf grown to his exacting specifications. I must have given him a withering look, because he meekly suggested, 'Well, we could use seed ... fast-growing seed. If we look after it, if the weather is kind, and we make sure it is properly watered, we might just be okay ...' He might well have added that he didn't under any circumstances recommend that course of action, but no doubt I had stopped listening by then!

I sold our turf to Chelsea.

As luck would have it, Alan decided to pop into my office for a chat during the close season. We talked about the things that had needed fixing for the upcoming season and I was doubtless very reassuring about the renewal of season tickets and corporate hospitality boxes. As you'll have seen from *The Apprentice*, Alan doesn't miss a trick and inevitably he wanted to have a look at how work was progressing with the relaying of the pitch.

I had omitted to mention my brilliant business transaction, having decided instead to announce it proudly at the next board meeting – by which time the seed would have grown, the pitch would be in a good state, and there would be universal acclaim for my canny piece of business.

I'm sure Alan walked out to the stadium with a picture in his mind of pristine green turf, bedded lovingly into the ground, ready to host our first match. We went out to the directors' box, Alan admired the large area of perfectly raked earth, and I explained in detail all the work that had taken place. I could see he was impressed.

'So when does the grass arrive?' he asked.

'Ah, well, what we have got is seed . . . very fast-growing seed.'

'What the ****! Are you ******* mad? Seriously, are you ******* mad!'

'We'll be all right, Alan, don't worry.'

'Claude, you do realise that if this pitch isn't ready for the start of the season, we are finished.'

The moment Alan left, I dashed over to see the groundsmen and told him to pray for sunshine . . . and for me!

I just about got away with it. Thank goodness our first game was away from home, giving an extra week of growth. By the third or fourth game of the season it was a genuinely fantastic playing surface, and the following season we won the award for best pitch in the league. For someone who is as risk-averse as me, it was one of my most stupid gambles. Trust me, given the same set of circumstances again, I wouldn't dream of taking that level of risk. I now shudder at the thought of it.

*

Being CEO of a Premier League club is not a job for the faint-hearted. Running a club like Spurs as a business means that everything you do is either wrong, crass or 'just not football'. Even if you make a decision that benefits the club, someone else usually takes the credit! I've written here about the administrative side of running the club. Dealing with the manager, players and players' agents is something else altogether!

It could only happen in football

In my early days at Spurs, it really was like a war zone. Over time, things settled and there was a better understanding amongst most of the stakeholders that we had established the building blocks for a solid business, and made great strides in professionalising the club and extending the brand franchise. Of course, the success of a football club is not measured by such things – it is results on the pitch that count – but by taking these steps we were ultimately able to get the club into a good position and sustain it.

Working with the two faces of the club always brought conflict – a match between the club and the company if you like. I felt confident sorting out the business side of things, but dealing with managers, players, agents and the coaching staff was a different matter. I've supported Tottenham all my life and, like any fan, when you come into close contact with your heroes, there may be a tendency to believe that their footballing brilliance will be matched by their personal qualities. In some instances, that was indeed the case, but for the most part it was not. One thing that I can confirm was that they were exceptionally talented athletes.

Jürgen Klinsmann – wonderful footballer, wonderful role model.

During one of the pre-season tours abroad, I had a unique opportunity to join in a training session and then a friendly with the first-team squad. Jürgen Klinsmann was in goal, and I was on Teddy Sheringham's team.

I was playing on the right side of defence. The Spurs left back, Justin Edinburgh, had the ball and was running towards me. Now, in my youth, I was a pretty impressive player (even if I say so myself) and I was confident that, given my 'silky skills', I would be able to deal with him. After all, I'd seen many times from the directors' box how easy it was for other players to dispossess him! He was getting closer, charging towards me. I had the measure of him. I was ready. By the time I had processed that thought, he had skipped past me. I couldn't believe the speed, power and skill. Since then, I have been careful to be respectful of every player's ability. They are superb footballers and amazing athletes.

While the players were, quite rightly, prized assets, they were kept wrapped in cotton wool and had everything done for them – and I mean *everything*. If we went on a trip, we had to gather all the passports before we went, otherwise many of the players would leave theirs at home. Sometimes it felt more like being on a school trip!

When I arrived in 1993, the manager was Ossie Ardiles – a club legend on my list of all-time great players and a former World Cup winner with Argentina. He had taken over under difficult circumstances and was doing his best, but the results just weren't coming through, despite some high-profile (and high-cost) players coming to the club. In October 1994, Alan decided that enough was enough and unfortunately had to move Ossie on. We got Gerry Francis from Queens Park Rangers – a former captain of England – in as our new manager.

In other businesses, when you replace a senior manager there is a more or less seamless transfer of authority – a one in, one out system. That's not how it works in football. Apart from the media interest, which is in itself disruptive, the new manager typically wants to bring in his own assistant manager and entourage of coaching staff – those who he has worked with before and trusts. This makes for a wholesale change: the old guard (who may not be that old) moves out, and the new complete unknowns move in. It doesn't stop there, of course, because the new manager will also want to bring in new players, which means offloading some of the existing players while negotiating to bring in new talent.

It is a merry-go-round, and makes a mockery of all our budgets and longer-term forecasts – another reason football is such a complicated business to run!

I got on well with Gerry Francis; we were mates and enjoyed a good working relationship. He was hard-working, experienced and respectful of the process of professional-ising the club, which Alan and I had established, and was

Spurs directors with legendary former team manager Bill Nicholson. From left to right: Colin Sandy, me, Douglas Alexiou, Alan Sugar, Bill Nicholson, Tony Berry and Igal Yawetz.

happy to go along with it. He also allowed me into the footballing side of things a lot more; he and Roger Cross, his assistant, made me feel part of the team, and for a time there was a spirit of collaboration between the business and the team. I was grateful and give Gerry a lot of credit for that, as many managers would not have been as accommodating. I also think it had a positive effect on the players and it certainly helped my rapport with them.

I went with Gerry on scouting missions and was involved in transfers. The first stage in the process of signing a targeted player is to obtain permission from his club to talk to him. There are all kinds of machinations that can go on during this phase, with players' agents 'stimulating' exchanges and the press speculating about targeted players. I have already mentioned how cosy clubs are with the press.

If this first hurdle is overcome, a transfer fee needs to be agreed in principle and then the player needs to be 'encouraged'. The players' agents normally have a strong say in this, as well as in negotiating and agreeing personal terms. Sometimes this process can happen very quickly, but usually there is a lot of toing and froing, and, if more than one club shows interest, things can get out of hand. I negotiated the transfer of Steffen Iversen, but we needed to be quick off the mark, as Liverpool FC had also apparently targeted the player and were making overtures.

On one occasion, we went to Bordeaux and Gerry saw a player he liked. The chairman of Bordeaux, Claude Bez, and I negotiated the deal for the player Gerry had identified. It was a done deal, other than the fact that the player Gerry was after came with a makeweight attached (an additional player that Bordeaux were looking to move on). This happens occasionally.

I explained to Gerry about having to take the other player as part of the deal, but he wasn't in the least interested in having the second player at the club. As far as I was concerned, it wasn't a big deal. Yes, we would have an extra player, and therefore extra wages to pay, but I felt we could, in turn, move him on in due course. And it wasn't costing us anything in terms of the transfer. The fee had been agreed for the player we wanted and this guy was a free add-on.

'No,' said Gerry. 'If we can't just buy the one player, then the deal is off.'

And that was that.

The makeweight's name? Zinedine Zidane – one of the greatest European players of the past few decades. Gerry felt he was too 'wooden'! It was a bit like turning down the Beatles or thinking that *Harry Potter* wouldn't sell. It happens in the music industry, in publishing, and in football – it's the nature of the game. Every single manager has made similar mistakes – there are no exceptions. Ferguson, Wenger, Mourinho ... all have missed great players (and bought a fair few overpriced flops).

Gerry was not a risk-taker, and he liked to work with players who he knew would deliver results. He brought in Les Ferdinand and David Ginola, both of whom were great.

Scouting another player, we went to Monaco on a number of occasions. After agreeing terms with the club, we took the target player out for dinner, and at the next table, I remember, were Ringo Starr and his wife. Eventually the player agreed to join us. Gerry was very excited. We sorted out the whole package – transfer fee, wages, everything.

Soon after, the player came to London to finalise the deal. The night before we were due to sign the contract, Gerry, Daniel Sugar and I went out for dinner with the player. We had a great evening! The player was scheduled to meet me in my office at 10.00 a.m. the following morning to sign the contract. At 9.00 a.m., Gerry phoned me.

'I don't want him. I've changed my mind.'

'But, Gerry, we've been to Monaco all those times. We've encouraged him. We've agreed the deal with him. He's a great player. Yesterday you loved him.'

'Sorry, Claude, but I've decided. I just don't fancy him.'

I called Alan, explained Gerry's position, and told him that the player was arriving in a few minutes.

'Well,' Alan suggested, 'maybe try to get him cheaper. That way perhaps we could sell him on for a profit, or at least break even if he doesn't work out.'

So the player came in and we sat down. 'Great,' I said. 'We are all ready to sign. Just to recap, this is the salary . . . ' I mentioned a number.

'No, wait. That's not what we agreed.'

'No, no, ah . . . perhaps you were thinking net. I was talking gross; maybe that has caused some confusion.' I felt sick to my stomach.

'I am going to have to think about this. I am going to speak to my friend Frank Leboeuf [a Chelsea player], and discuss this with him and I will let you know.' With that, he left. We ordered and paid for his taxi.

He didn't head for Leboeuf or Chelsea, though. He went

straight to Arsène Wenger, the manager at Arsenal, and that afternoon David Dein (the Arsenal vice-chairman) called Alan Sugar and told him Arsenal were going to sign the player. Of course, the next day the papers were full of the story that Spurs had been snubbed. The player? Emmanuel Petit.

Football works in mysterious ways, and with the amount of money now available through the Sky TV deal, things could rapidly get out of control. For instance, there was another time when Gerry had identified a player with a price tag of £700,000. 'Fine,' I said, 'I'll do the deal.'

I contacted the club, only to discover that they had recently sold the player to an Italian club. No problem. I went to Italy to meet with the chairman and explained that we'd like to buy the player. He'd only played one or two games for them by this point. Gerry had already indicated that he thought the player was good value at a million pounds and that's what I offered.

'Oh no, I couldn't sell this guy for one million. He's worth one and a half.'

'No, I'm afraid we can't stretch to that. I know you bought him for seven hundred thousand so that is more than double. Thanks, but that's too much.'

I stayed for a great game that evening, left Milan the following morning, and told Gerry the deal was off.

'Look, Claude, I've been thinking. I think he is worth every bit of two million.'

'But, Gerry, we originally said seven hundred thousand, and now you are talking two million.'

'I think he's worth it.'

So I contacted the chairman and told him we could do the

deal at £1.7 million. But now the price was £2.3 million. At the next match, I relayed all this to Alan.

'This is getting ridiculous, Alan,' I said. 'Now he wants two point three million.'

'Leave it to me, Claude. I'll sort it out.'

In the end we paid £2.7 million. There was nothing wrong with the player – he was good enough – but we ended up paying way over the odds, because we had lost the upper hand in the negotiations. You have to be strong and positive in these situations.

But for all my involvement in the transfers, and my good relations with the manager, there was still a division between the football and administrative sides. Things tended to move along fine until the moment you challenged the manager or the players. There was a quantity of small expenses claims that were being charged to the club and I questioned them all. This drove the manager mad, but I just wouldn't allow some to go through.

On one occasion, one of the youth teams was playing a tournament abroad, accompanied by the coaching staff. It was great experience for the young lads to play against continental opposition. On their return, as usual, I checked through the expenses receipts and came across one for a set of new golf clubs. I summoned the claimant, a member of the coaching staff, and he explained that he had taken his golf clubs along and that British Airways must have lost them on the flight home, since they had never arrived. So he'd just bought a new set and wanted to be reimbursed!

What exactly did that have to do with Tottenham Hotspur? And why had he brought his clubs with him in the first place? He was there to work, not for a holiday. I didn't pay the bill. It felt in many respects that there was a culture of 'take, take, take' and I was determined to put a stop to it.

Looking back, I believe that I got the big decisions right and dealt with the larger problems well. I was instrumental in ensuring that the income generated from all our activities ended up in the company bank account, as well as refocusing everyone's attention on operating efficiently. We had good processes in place, and the financial wherewithal and ambition to bring in top players – and to win.

I negotiated multi-million-pound sponsorship deals, secured the contract to play NFL American football during our close season, moved the club to all-ticket sales, oversaw the building of two new stands (on time and on budget), and developed the merchandise division into a lucrative profit centre. In the years I was there, I professionalised every aspect of the operational running of the club and the company.

I think where I fell down was in being too hasty to change things. If I'd taken longer to assess the problems before charging in, I would have realised that I needed to be very wary of public scrutiny and the club culture before making drastic changes. I might have found a way of working that alienated fewer people and maintained the clubby atmosphere, while supporting it with a framework of serious business.

For me, the clear priority is always to get the job done. It is essential to put a stop to wasteful or counterproductive practices and ensure that the company has a future. Focusing on the business issues will also flush out those who are not committed, have little interest in working hard, or just don't have the ability to do the job that is required of them. It also establishes if the company has good future prospects or needs to be simply prettied up and sold on.

*

I truly enjoyed the challenge of being involved with Spurs. What an unbelievable privilege. I could almost repeat the words of the TV apprentices: 'Thank you, Lord Sugar, for the opportunity.' I also loved spending weekends with my wife and children at White Hart Lane, and being involved with the Sugar family and other board members when we travelled to the away games.

I am still fascinated by the football industry. It is full of passion, energy, scandal, intrigue and absurdity. The money at the top level is ludicrous, and the Sky production of live matches is spectacular. But do I want to get back into football? No, thank you − been there, done that, have the T-shirt, and bear the scars.

In the autumn of 1997, my work at Tottenham Hotspur was by no means over, but one day, out of the blue, the course of my life changed and I embarked on my greatest challenge yet.

Lifesavers

As I write, I've known and worked with Alan Sugar for about twenty-five years. Since those early days at Amstrad France and Spain, I've grown to respect him as a man of exceptional ability and someone who genuinely inspires admiration. He is a strong character – not blessed with suave charm like Richard Branson, say – but he is incredibly decisive, straight and to the point.

On so many occasions, when we are faced with difficult situations, Alan comes up with the simplest, most obvious and effective solutions. I smile to myself at the sheer brilliance of his thought process, and kick myself for not having come up with it before him. He is loyal and has that rare gift of engendering loyalty in others. He also has a sixth sense about business, people's abilities and how they might fit into a role or a company – which, of course, makes him ideal for, amongst other things, *The Apprentice*.

What I have found is that, for the most part, we are on the same wavelength, although I might well have a different way of managing or resolving business issues. I am not sure how it has come about, but I seem to be one of a small group of people he turns to when he needs something sorted out, or reassurance that he has got his facts straight. I have only ever had a couple of genuine disagreements with Alan in all the years we have worked together. One of them occurred at Tottenham in October 1997, and it saved my life.

For whatever reason – I think various members of staff had been bending his ear – Alan arrived, unannounced, at my office to sort it out. He was completely wound up and venting his displeasure at me. We were both pacing up and down the two sides of the long meeting-room table, arguing the point. Believe it or not, I have absolutely no recollection of what the disagreement was about.

I thought he was wrong, but could see there was no way to pacify him or reason with him, and I wasn't going to yield, either. He had somehow got the wrong end of the stick. After a few minutes I had had enough, packed up my briefcase and, without another word, walked out. I also switched my phone off, knowing that the one thing Alan really hates is being unable to contact someone.

Under normal circumstances, I don't shy away from a good old row and, if confronted and riled, my blood boils and I absolutely go for the jugular. I can't stop myself – it's just the way I am. On this occasion, though, I held back, did the sensible thing, and just walked away.

Now faced with a day off, I decided to take advantage of it and make an appointment with my GP. I had been aware of the symptoms of a hernia for some time and thought I might as well get it sorted. I explained to the doctor that

I knew I would probably need a minor procedure. He had a look. 'Ah, no. I don't think you have a hernia.'

'Yes, I do. I know about these things. Players suffer from them from time to time.'

'No, that is not a hernia. I think you need to go and see someone.'

'Fine. All I need is someone who knows about hernias.'

The GP made a call to a specialist and told me to go straight there. The specialist told me to take off my shirt and lie down on the bed. He proceeded to move the ultrasound scanner over my chest, and I could see the image of my heart on the monitor.

'Well, Mr Littner, your heart is very healthy. I can also see that you have never smoked – your lungs are in excellent condition.' Yes, I was thinking, and this is a bloody waste of time! Then he moved the scanner a bit lower. 'Oh dear.'

And with that, he turned the screen away from my line of sight. He felt my abdomen. 'That is definitely not a hernia.' He then arranged an immediate visit to another specialist, where I was given an MRI scan and had some blood tests.

The specialist sat me down. 'Mr Littner, you have cancer.'

The next day I was scheduled to have a meeting with an oncologist. I asked the Tottenham doctor, Mark Curtin, to come with me, just so I had someone there who would understand exactly what was being said. We were introduced to Professor David Linch, an eminent oncologist at University College Hospital, who escorted us into a very small room. I remember it being hot, stuffy and airless.

In a single breath, Professor Linch said, 'Mr Littner, you

have non-Hodgkin's lymphoma. You have six months to live.'

Mark Curtin fainted. I didn't feel that great either.

Had it not been for the fateful argument with Alan, there is no way I would have gone to the doctor that day. There hadn't seemed to be anything urgent about my 'hernia' – I felt absolutely fine in myself – so I would probably have left it weeks or months, which would almost certainly have meant that the diagnosis would have come too late to save me.

Non-Hodgkin's lymphoma (NHL) is a kind of blood cancer. Lymphomas, in general, are cancers that start in the lymphatic system. If you have NHL, certain types of white blood cells in your lymphatic system become abnormal; they multiply and collect around glands and other parts of the lymphatic system, causing tumours to form. In my case, they had gathered in my groin and stomach, where I had a grapefruit-sized tumour.

After dropping the initial bombshell, Professor Linch went on to urge me to take a course of chemotherapy as a way of possibly extending my life. It was abundantly clear that my next challenge wasn't going to be a professional one.

Alan reacted in a way that I'll always remember. When I switched my phone on again after those traumatic couple of days, there were, of course, numerous voicemail messages from him. He was shocked and upset when he heard the news. His immediate reaction was: 'Just get better, Claude.' Those words resonated strongly and were expressed with sensitivity. Alan demonstrated a light touch and did not make a 'drama out of a crisis'. I really appreciated that.

At the beginning of my treatment, I still felt fine physically, so I carried on going to the office. The thing about undergoing chemotherapy is that it is progressively debilitating. After the first round of injections, I felt fine. I had been told it would be terrible, but felt all right. I thought, This is a doddle. After the second round, yes, I felt a little more tired. And by the third or fourth session, it was awful.

I remember clearly the moment when I realised that carrying on working just wasn't possible. I was sitting in a meeting with John Sedgwick, Spurs' finance director. He had brought me the draft management accounts to go through with him, prior to circulating them to the board in advance of the monthly meeting. I was always very keen to review the numbers, challenge anything that seemed out of line, and highlight any issues I felt needed particular attention.

We began working through the forty or so pages of the accounts – second nature to me – but somehow things were different. The pages were a complete blur. The numbers meant nothing. I couldn't interpret or understand anything. I wasn't able to function. I wasn't myself. I wasn't in control . . . I burst into tears.

John excused himself, went back down to his office and must have phoned Alan to tell him I wasn't 'all the ticket', because, within a few moments, my phone rang. It was Alan.

'Listen, Claude, I want you to go home. Right now. And I don't want you to come back until you are well. First of all, this is not good for you – and it's not good for the staff either. I've already told you to concentrate on getting better. That is the priority. Don't worry about your job. I will keep it open for you as long as necessary.'

Typical Alan – get straight to the point and address the

problem. At the time, I remember thinking that I wished he had said come back in a couple of days, but he was absolutely right, of course – I needed to focus on beating the cancer. Alan realised that it would not be possible for me to continue as chief executive. Indeed, working was no longer an option. To all intents and purposes, that really was my exit from Tottenham Hotspur. My departure was as abrupt as my arrival.

I was forty-seven years old – in my prime, so to speak, in business terms – and had thought I would be able to carry on. Being told not to come back really took something away from me. What had my life come to? To be honest, up until that moment, I hadn't really grasped just how perilous my situation was. I had felt mostly okay. I had always felt that I was going to be all right. Sure, I lacked a bit of energy and felt nauseous most of the time, but basically I didn't think too much of it. This is me we are talking about – I am very tough – but that conversation brought home to me just what a desperate situation I was in, and it was psychologically hard on me.

Before I knew it, my life revolved around daily appointments and eventually admission as an in-patient to University College Hospital (UCH), where I received numerous treatments of high-dose chemotherapy. The months I spent in hospital were miserable, even though I had amazing support from my parents, my wonderful wife Thelma, my sons Anthony and Alex, and my wider family.

Every morning my mother would come to the hospital and sit with me for the whole day. My father would visit in the morning, go to work, and pop in again on his way home in the evening. Thelma was running back and forth to the hospital with lunch and dinner, on the off chance that I might perhaps feel like eating something, and would then spend the evening with me. My children would also come in to see me every weekend, and made sure they came home from university to be with me. The nurses were absolutely wonderful – so caring, cheerful and friendly. I defy anyone to say anything bad about the nursing fraternity; they kept me going and their patience and kindness knew no bounds.

On one occasion I had to go to a unit called Nuclear Medicine. I had always been determined that I was never going to be wheeled anywhere in a wheelchair, even though I was so very weak that I could barely walk. The route to that department in another area of the hospital was via an underground walkway, past the morgue. Progress was very, very slow, but it was not like I had anything else to do that day! Eventually, I arrived.

As I sat, waiting to be called, I looked at all the other patients in the waiting room – very sick people – and thought, God, these people look almost dead. Then I realised, Oh my God. *I* look like that!

You start to look like an alien – no hair at all, no eyebrows or eyelashes, a sunken face and a bowed back. You barely look human at all. But when you are in your hospital bed you don't realise the state you are in.

Also, when you are as ill as I was, you have no power left and no say in anything. The doctor comes to see you when he wants to – not when you ask him to. Even out of hospital, I was powerless. I had to see the doctor whenever he specified. I couldn't just go away for a week – not if they had been doing tests and were expecting the results.

I would be told, 'You aren't going anywhere. You are coming in tomorrow.' It is a very different way to live your life and not one that I relished for a moment – I like to be in charge and make my own decisions. Here I had no control over anything.

The nurses would come in, give me my chemotherapy, then go, and I just accepted all that. I went with the flow. Whatever they wanted to do with me, they could do it. I was passive. In all the companies I have gone into, and in my personal life, I had control, authority, power. Now, I wasn't making any decisions, and it did give me a different perspective on life. What was going to happen was going to happen. That was my attitude. But deep down, I always thought I was going to survive. I think that inner strength, when my physical strength was gone, gave me the courage to keep going.

With so many injections and drugs being pumped into me, there was no way that my veins could withstand that amount of punishment. I was therefore fitted with something called a Hickman line. In fact, over the period of my illness, I had a number of them fitted under general anaesthetic and then removed.

In essence – this bit is not for the squeamish – catheter lumens (tubes) are inserted into your chest and fed subcutaneously into the jugular vein. This makes it easy to administer the chemotherapy, and any other drugs, and blood can easily be withdrawn for analysis. I do find it very hard to talk about this even now. In some ways, the memory of those wretched Hickman lines, the constant attachment, cleaning and administering of drugs – wired up like some sort of artificial being – is one of the most difficult. I can still remember the sensation of touching the lines under my skin. And I shudder when I do.

The sensation of being at the mercy of other people was very uncomfortable and, on at least one occasion, downright dangerous. One night, when I was fast asleep in my hospital bed, exhausted from the battering my body was taking, I had the feeling that someone had come in, given me chemo and was now draining the blood to make sure the line was not blocked. Then, a while later, an agency nurse came into the room. What struck me for some reason, when she put down the tray containing the cocktail of drugs, was that she had long, painted fingernails. 'I am just here to give you your chemotherapy,' she said. But somewhere in my mind I knew I had already had my dose.

'No, no. I've just had that.'

She tut-tutted. 'Don't be difficult, Mr Smith!'

'No. *No*. I'm not Mr Smith – he's next door.'

She just picked up her tray and walked out. Whatever she was going to administer, it wasn't meant for me! Scary. I could barely remember anything then, but something in the back of my mind had kept me alert enough to remember that I had undergone the treatment already.

After many months of treatment, I was sent for a PET scan (a kind of radioactive, three-dimensional imaging technique used for disease diagnosis) as the doctors couldn't understand why the tumour wasn't shrinking. They had been blasting my body with chemotherapy, but, it seemed, to no effect. The PET scan revealed that there was no blood supply to the tumour; it was just sitting there, dead, which explained why it wasn't shrinking . . . or growing.

It was, therefore, safe for them to operate on me and cut it out.

Following the operation, I was on a morphine drip for the pain. All I had to do, and was encouraged to do regularly, was press a button placed in the palm of my hand, and that would release a measured dose, but I didn't press the button once. I wanted, above all, to have my wits about me. I wanted to be in control of my brain, and I knew that the morphine would remove the pain, but also the control. I wanted to remain alert enough to know what was going on. It was absurd, really, not to press the button, but that is my determination and single-mindedness again.

I had a nurse watching over me all night long, and had the strangest feeling that I had died at some point in the night, but of course I couldn't have, because I woke up the following morning. I got through all the treatment and had an autologous stem-cell transplant using my own stem cells previously extracted from my bone marrow.

At the end of it all, I was okay. I beat the cancer, and was in remission.

It was now 1999, and Alan asked me to oversee a legal case involving Amstrad in California – nothing arduous and, of course, the perfect place to recuperate. I came back to the UK when the work was done.

Unfortunately, the cancer returned, too. I developed more tumours. This meant a return to high-dose chemotherapy to arrest the spread of the cancer and kill it off. Apparently, my own stem cells weren't effective at attacking the abnormal cells. At one point, it became clear that the only option left to me was a new treatment, which used donor stem cells. I was one of the first people to undergo this treatment, which required a particular concoction of drugs, coupled with cells from a donor who was a very good match in tissue types. Therein lay the problem: from the worldwide database, there did not appear to be a good tissue match for me. In something approaching desperation, David Linch asked if I had any siblings. As it happens, I have a sister, Tina. They tested her and, by an absolute miracle, the match was near perfect.

I was in the last-chance saloon: my own stem cells hadn't protected me from the formation of cancerous tumours, and there was no firm basis for believing that Tina's would. In fact, I remember going to a New Year's Eve party at the end of 1999 – the end of one millennium and the threshold of a new one – and entertaining the passing thought that I might die in the coming year.

The first part of the procedure involved my sister having a course of injections to stimulate the production of her stem cells. Veins in each of her arms were then connected by tubes to a cell separator machine. The blood flowed from one arm into the separator and then back again into the other arm.

Meanwhile, I had completed my course of high-dose chemotherapy to destroy the existing bone marrow and my cancer cells and stop my immune system working. Tina's stem cells were then slowly fed into my body via the Hickman line. I then had to wait for the stem cells to settle in my bone marrow and start producing new blood cells. To cut to the chase, if the stem cells do not start to produce new blood cells, and if your body rejects them, you die. If not, you live ... probably.

I try to keep memories of that time suppressed. It was incredibly difficult. There were numerous unpleasant side-effects that stayed with me for some considerable time as my body tried to reject my sister's stem cells. This is called graft-versus-host disease. Where my cells reacted against

With my family on the touchline at Spurs
during a period of remission.

my sister's cells, my skin became very scaley and would peel off. Even in weak sunshine, I would burn. I was always freezing cold.

I remember one morning, a few months after the treatment, I woke up to find my whole body covered in warts. I was rushed to hospital and put in the isolation unit until they could work out what was wrong. No one knew whether I'd contracted some rare disease or whether it was a reaction to the treatment. I ended up staying in that room for six weeks. I couldn't have any visitors, because as long as the hospital didn't know what I had, there was a chance it could be something contagious. The warts eventually disappeared, and I was released from solitary confinement. Sisters . . . nothing but trouble!

At the end of it all, I was alive. I weighed less than nine stone. But I was alive.

*

I have been free of cancer since March 2000. I went for monthly check-ups for years, and each time half expected to hear that they had found another tumour. Life felt precarious – in some ways it still does, because I don't think you can ever be that close to the end of it and not feel vulnerable about something over which you have no control. But I am now down to having annual check-ups with my wonderful oncologist and friend, David Linch. Even now, though, I chat to him for as long as I can before he gives me the results of the blood test. While I am anxious to hear the news, I just don't want it to be bad.

It is an extraordinary time to look back on, and I am very

emotional as I recount this part of my life, during which time I had no control and no idea of what was going to happen, and every single plan I had made had to be discarded. My illness impacted deeply on the lives of my loved ones, and I can only try and make up for that by being a better person every day.

Did the experience change me? How could it not? I have been given a different perspective on life. I am now very sensitive to others who are facing serious illness, and try to be helpful to those who are enduring similar experiences to mine.

A friend of mine rang me one day and told me that Peter Hunt, the brother of the racing driver James Hunt, was going through a really rough time. He had myeloma, a rare form of blood cancer, which is similar to, but rarer than, NHL. So I called him and we had regular chats, and, in a gallows humour way, a bit of a laugh.

At the end of one of our conversations, he asked me to join him on the board of the Myeloma UK cancer charity. We used to sit together at meetings, a bit like naughty schoolchildren – *fond de la classe* again! – and laugh a lot, but sadly his condition grew worse and he passed away.

*

When asked, I willingly talk to people with NHL when things get rough. I hope they get some comfort and hope from the fact that I have survived this long after coming so close to the end. I try to give them the courage and strength to see it through, and have occasionally managed to make them laugh and make light of some of the most unpleasant and distressing moments and side-effects.

I didn't want to look back, though. What I wanted was to get back in the game as quickly as possible. The question was, how?

Getting back on track

Back in March 1997, I had been invited to attend a lunch on the theme of 'The Governance of Sport' at the Institute of Economic Affairs, which I'd thought might be interesting. As it turned out, it wasn't at all! However, I had been seated next to Denis Thatcher and we had had a nice little chat.

I had been conscious throughout the event that the chap sitting on the other side of Denis was listening in on our conversation. He'd seemed very keen to catch my attention, but I'd had no idea who he was, and hadn't spoken to him.

A few days later, I received a call from someone called Simon Bentley. He introduced himself as the gentleman who had been sitting alongside Denis Thatcher. He was chairman and chief executive of Blacks Leisure plc, the outdoor and sportswear retailer, as well as a lifelong supporter of Spurs and, according to him, a great admirer of mine!

He asked if we might meet for lunch, as he had a business

proposition to put to me. To cut a long story short, he was keen for me to join Blacks as a non-executive director. Blacks sounded like a very interesting company and Simon struck me as a very astute businessman. However, at that time I was fully engaged as CEO of Spurs and unfortunately had to decline the opportunity.

Fast forward eighteen months or so to when I'd got through the first phase of my illness, and well before the reappearance of the cancer towards the end of 1999. Although I was not at full strength, I wanted to get back to work. Alan was taking a somewhat different view, though. He appointed me a non-executive director at Spurs – not exactly what I was looking for, but they had restructured and there was no longer a CEO role in the set-up. Alan himself had taken a more hands-on role and both Daniel Sugar and John Sedgwick, the finance director, had also widened their remits.

The press release issued by Alan, in his capacity as chairman, read as follows:

> *Claude Littner was appointed chief executive five years ago at a time when the company needed his business acumen and management skills to develop the financial and commercial framework of the company. Having met all his objectives, Mr Littner will now seek a new executive challenge outside the Group, but will maintain an involvement as a non-executive director of the plc and Football Club. As a consequence, I will take a more active hands-on interest in the day-to-day management of the business. The board wishes Claude well and thanks him for his total dedication and successful stewardship of the company.*

Very shortly after Alan's announcement, I received another call from Simon Bentley. He was still very keen for me to join the board of Blacks Leisure, and, in view of my new non-executive role at Spurs, felt sure that I would now have the time to consider his proposal. For my part, it sounded like a wonderful business and an exciting opportunity – exactly the kind of thing I was really looking for.

We met on a number of occasions, and I also met with all the other members of the board. At that time, the company had three UK store formats: First Sport, Blacks Outdoor and AV (Active Venture), with some 220 stores nationwide. Blacks Leisure also held the exclusive UK distribution rights for the O'Neill sport and fashion brand, as well as a forty per cent shareholding in Fila (UK) Ltd, and the exclusive UK licence and distribution rights for the Fila sports fashion brands.

In June 1999 I took my place on the board of Blacks Leisure as a non-executive director, joining what was an impressive line-up: Simon Bentley as chairman and chief executive, Andy Hall as finance director, Tom Knight as managing director of First Sport's Sport and Fashion division, and Sir Rhodes Boyson, Donald Trangmar and David Bernstein as fellow non-executive directors.

For the first few board meetings, I sat there wondering how I was ever going to justify my presence there. These guys were really smart, and Simon was on the ball and led from the front.

In, or around, September that same year, the board got together to discuss a possible acquisition of the Outdoor Group, which comprised the Millets and Free Spirit fascias, the UK's largest retailer of outdoor clothing, footwear and

equipment. Don Trangmar, who had been a main board
director of Marks & Spencer, was influential and very keen
on the deal. In November, we did the deal for £50.8 million. At a stroke, Blacks became the clear UK market leader
in the outdoor retail sector. Very exciting stuff, although
my contribution was still, at best, negligible. The group
was reorganised into two distinct divisions: the Outdoor
Division and the Sports and Fashion Division. In total, we
had some three hundred stores nationwide. Roy Crosland,
the chief executive of Millets, was to run the Outdoor
Division and join the main board, with Tom Knight running the Sports and Fashion Division as the appointed
deputy chairman.

Over time, I combined my duties at Blacks with other
roles – principally Powerleague and ASCO (more about both
of those in the following chapters), as well as Norton Way
Motors, Cyan Technology and Azzurri. At that point, from
the end of 1999 to the early 2000s, Blacks was particularly
interesting for me – not only because I was back in a retail
environment, but also because I got to see up close what
happens when you put the wrong people in top jobs.

As I mentioned, when I joined, Simon Bentley was
chairman and chief executive. He was very smart and we
got on very well. Then, in January 2000, tragedy struck –
Simon had a terrible skiing accident and, as a result, was
going to be out of action for an indeterminate period of
time.

At that point I had health issues of my own to contend
with and was in hospital, away from Blacks, for some four
months. On my return, I found that there had been a power
shift, and the board had come to the conclusion that it was

imperative to appoint a new chairman. I disagreed, on the basis that Simon would be returning, and argued that we should hold off on making any changes.

David Bernstein appeared to have the confidence of the other board members, but stated that he would only take on the chairman's role if the board voted him in unanimously. I didn't give him my vote, but David agreed to accept the majority decision anyway, and became the new chairman. That event, despite appearances, did not cause a rift – it was simply taken as a difference of opinion. But, perhaps due to the parallels with the fate of my own position at Spurs during my illness, I was more sensitive to the situation, and felt that the board had been precipitous in appointing a new chairman.

David turned out to have a very consensual style, and, under his chairmanship, gave board members ample opportunity to express their views. However, after a year had passed, Simon was ready to return. He wasn't the same, though: he was less confident and appeared less able. Notwithstanding that, I thought he would get better over time and wanted him to retake the chair. David wouldn't step aside, though, and had the support of the other members of the board. David told me that if I wanted Simon back, he could return as chief executive.

I didn't think Simon was strong enough for that role; it was too full-on, too stressful and probably beyond him at that point in time. But that was all that the board would agree to. I was nominated to put the offer to Simon, and he accepted the position and returned as chief executive.

I should point out that, in the year that Simon was away from the business, the company's share price had gone from

350p to 175p and, on his return, his first task was to issue a profits warning, as the normally buoyant Christmas sales period had been awful. This was followed by an abysmal period of trading as a direct result of the outbreak of foot-and-mouth disease, during which ten million sheep and cattle were killed in an attempt to halt the spread of the contagion. As the UK's leading outdoor and camping retailer, this had a dramatic impact on Blacks' sales.

Then, quite out of the blue, in March 2001, it became known to the Blacks board that Tom Knight had been touting interest from venture capital firms to secure the backing to bid for Blacks Leisure plc. Tom confirmed this, which immediately put him in a conflicted position, and he was excluded from any board discussions on that subject. More importantly, it caused a real rift in the board. We felt betrayed, and, crucially, it alerted the market to the vulnerable position Blacks was in, making us a potential takeover target. In the end, Tom was unable to mount a bid, and, for a short while, the board tried to get back to normality and put the aberration behind us.

Then, almost without pausing for breath, Blacks opened a further thirty-two stores and refurbished others. The group also acquired forty-seven outlets from the administrative receivers of Famous Army Stores Ltd. All of this sounded great, but the key was to ensure that all this activity actually yielded it profit. It didn't! What it did do was put a huge strain on the bank facility, already stretched due to the previous year's poor trading.

The retail landscape in outdoor and sportswear was beginning to take shape in my mind, with JD Sports serving the higher end of the retail branded market, Sports Direct owning the lower end, and Blacks and JJB somewhat stuck in the middle ground.

We decided that we needed to apply some focus to the business and resolved to dispose of the Sports and Fashion Division to JD Sports. This meant that Tom Knight would leave the group. There had been an uncomfortable truce at board level ever since Tom's 'betrayal' and no one was sorry about the *coup de grâce*. However, the board had also arrived at an uncomfortable truth about Simon Bentley, deciding that the role was proving too much for him. David Bernstein said that, as I was the one who had insisted on his return, I should also be the one to give him the bad news. He had conveniently forgotten that I had wanted Simon back as chairman, not CEO.

Having weathered these turbulent times, Roy Crosland became group chief executive, which made perfect sense since he was an excellent retailer and the group was now heavily focused on the outdoor market, where we had a clear market advantage and, in Roy, an excellent operator. For the next two years, the group produced year-on-year increases in turnover and profit, with a strong focus on outdoor, under the Millets and Blacks fascias, and onboardwear under the O'Neill and Free Spirit fascias.

Roy eventually left to pursue private interests at the end of 2004, and an external candidate, Russell Hardy, was appointed in his place. Russell was an exuberant character and David often remarked on how dynamic and motivational he was, and we both noted the marked difference between Roy's and Russell's management styles. Where Roy had been cautious, reserved and, frankly, rather boring,

Russell was optimistic, forthright and over the top. Roy kept things close to his chest, whereas Russell could not wait to get everything out in the open. He was also passionate about delivering the products, services and store environment. His strategic plan was built around five key components: product development, format development, brand communication, operational efficiency and business development. Once Russell had set out his strategy, he really went for it.

He introduced a new, high-performance 'Technicals' range for men and an outdoor fitness range – 'Rare Species' – for women, relaunched a 'lifestyle' travel range in Blacks under the 'ALS' (Air, Land, Sea) label, and started a new 'Equator' trekking range in Millets, along with a new 'Free Spirit' range for women.

Board meetings became a forum for fashion shows, where the board were deluged with multiple new ranges from over-enthusiastic designers who had been given free rein. Don Trangmar was sceptical and I also had heated discussions with David about the number of new ranges being introduced. The price points were beginning to make me feel queasy as well: they were uncompetitive when set against the leading brands. I became more and more set against the new ranges, and by the time the new out-of-town format of Blacks stores was rolled out, I was convinced we were heading in the wrong direction.

My issues with the new clothing ranges paled into insignificance compared with my reservations about the new stores. The leases were horrendous, the fit-out costs diabolical, and the stock, although beautifully merchandised, was not attracting customers. I recall being in a car with David and Don on one occasion and refusing to let them out before I had completed my rant about how these new stores were 'killing us'. I remember, in the end, summarising that the locations were wrong, the format was wrong, the merchandise was wrong – in short, everything was a catastrophe! I was seeing *red*! And to top it all, Russell was talking about opening another ten of these monstrosities. David's simple response was: 'We either back him or sack him.' That wasn't the point I was making – the point was that we needed to curtail and monitor these myriad activities.

Whilst all these changes were going on, the board took a further costly strategic decision to vacate the four cramped warehouses and makeshift offices that we had been operating from during Roy's stewardship, and undertook the building work for a new head office and warehouse.

Despite everything, in the financial year ending 28 February 2006, sales were up, as were profits. I'm sure many of the other board members wondered what I was being so awkward for!

On the face of it, Blacks was in good shape. We had a commanding position in the outdoor market and, with health and fitness and outdoor life becoming something of a strong trend, and boardwear and high-fashion surf brands growing ever more popular, Blacks looked well positioned to prosper. Having said that, our sales were very weather dependent. From my own retail experience, when it rained, sales of umbrellas shot up, but no rain . . . zero sales.

During the warm and dry spring weather of 2007, Millets' sales nosedived, compounding what had been a very poor Christmas period in 2006. It was something of a perfect storm (if only it had actually rained), since so much investment had been put into the new ranges, new-format stores, and the move to the new warehouse. We closed forty-five loss-making stores and began to exit onerous leases. Guess which some of those were? Coincidentally and perversely, Blacks won the Best New Out of Town award from *Retail Week* magazine.

The financial situation in 2007 did not look good. Our stock levels were significantly higher than normal, and the previous year's operating profit of £22 million had turned into a £12 million loss by the year ending 3 March 2007. Too late in the day, David realised that the strategy we had unwittingly subscribed to was horribly flawed, and our timing could not have been worse.

Over the years, I had become very friendly with David. We always travelled together to and from our board meetings at Blacks in Northampton, and we had the most interesting conversations on a wide range of topics. David is worldly, mature and knowledgeable. However, no journey was complete without me taking him to task about the way Blacks was being managed. He could see the strength of my arguments, but I felt he was painfully slow to react. His style, as I have already mentioned, was one of seeking the board's collective view on a range of topics, and then not necessarily concluding by making a prompt decision.

In June 2007, Russell Hardy resigned from the board and, over the next few months, David and I interviewed a number of individuals who were put forward by a specialist recruitment agency. It is hard for me to express my exasperation with some of these high-flying, corporate wallies. On one occasion, I asked one of these numpties what his greatest accomplishment had been in his previous job. Without a moment's thought, he replied that he had moved the escalator to ease the flow of footfall. At this point I kicked David under the desk to indicate that the interview could be quickly terminated.

Eventually, we met with Neil Gillis, and he was appointed in November 2007. Neil was impressive, a real smooth talker who always spoke calmly and with authority. He made a bright start, I suppose, and spent the first couple of months visiting the estate and getting to grips with the situation. During his first board meeting, we were subjected to a lengthy slide show demonstrating the deplorable state of many of the shops, and the poor level of control and discipline at branch level. We saw dirty windows, rubbish boxes piled outside the shops, shop signs that had fallen off. Neil declared that a radical change was necessary. Oh no, not another one, I thought!

Neil correctly reduced overheads at the head office, mainly in merchandising and HR, and put in place a more flexible working pattern in store, which focused on staff being present during the peak trading times. He set out his strategy to dress the shop windows with dry- and wet-weather formats, so that they could be changed depending on the weather outlook. He cut the ranges and trialled a new and more contemporary way to reflect the quality and desirability of the products. These tests were carried out in our High Street Kensington and Holborn stores in London – hardly representative of the estate – and Neil claimed success. In boardwear, he also introduced a programme of rationalisation.

At a time when I felt strongly that we needed a very hands-on chief executive, I found Neil to be remote and unengaged. He always presented himself as a self-assured 'Mr Perfect', and David gave him the benefit of the doubt, despite the concerns I expressed about his ability or where-withal to effect a turnaround.

As 2008 wore on, it was increasingly apparent that, for all this endeavour, Blacks was going downhill. The economic downturn was upon us, and I was absolutely sure we were caught between a rock and a hard place.

I met with David privately and expressed my deep anxiety, stressing that we were in big trouble with an under-performing management team. David was sympathetic but kept pointing out that 'We had a good Saturday last week, Claude' or offering reassurances, such as: 'Claude, you'll see. It's all going to be fine.'

I told David that our only hope was to sell the company. 'No, no, no', came his response. 'We'll be all right.'

Months went by with more consolations such as 'we had a good Saturday', or Bank Holiday, but these were temporary, short-term boosts, which, to my mind, couldn't disguise that the fundamentals of the business were badly wrong. We were in a hole and, for the life of me, I just could not see how we were going to get out – certainly not with the management team we currently had in place.

I repeated my concerns to David: 'It's not looking good to me. The strategy isn't working and it's our reputation on the line now. We've been here a while. You are chairman and I am now deputy chairman. It's happening on our watch. The business is floundering.' The banks were also beginning to put pressure on, and limiting out facility.

I decided to act. I told David that I was going to speak to Simon Bentley, now chairman at Sports Direct plc, a fully quoted sports retailer on the London Stock Exchange, to have an off-the-record conversation to see if there might possibly be any interest in them acquiring Blacks Leisure. David wasn't happy, but agreed. I spoke to Simon, who relayed the question to Sports Direct's founder and principal shareholder, Mike Ashley. Some days later, Mike asked to meet me, saying that he could be interested in buying Blacks, but *only* Blacks. He didn't want Millets.

I reported back to David. 'We've got a result here. Blacks is the fascia that is giving us grief. In fact, we are losing our shirts with Blacks. Millets is still pretty good, a Steady Eddie. Let them buy Blacks. This is our get out of jail free card.'

David replied, 'I don't think so, Claude. If he wants to buy it, he has to take the whole thing.'

'David, let's not piss this bloke around,' I said. 'Sports Direct would not have a funding problem acquiring the Blacks fascia. If he wants to buy just the Blacks format, let him.' But I went back to Mike and told him what David had insisted upon.

Time passed, sales were still going down and the Blacks share price continued to fall. The banks were increasing the pressure. Somewhat to my surprise, Mike eventually came back and said he would consider buying the whole group.

In these types of situations, it is normal to incentivise shareholders to accept the offer by paying a premium over the prevailing share price, and Mike suggested he would do exactly that. I went back to David and gave him the news.

David said 'no'.

'What do you mean? This is our chance. We can exit this business with our reputations intact, and pass it to a substantial company who can invest and has the financial and management capability to fix it.'

'No, he has to make a higher offer.'

'David, we're in a hole here. That is a fair offer and a decent premium over our current share price.'

'No, tell him he needs to offer more.'

'David, there may be more bad news to come out of Blacks. Now is the time to get the ball rolling, not to play hardball.' But David was adamant.

More months went by. Our share price came under further pressure. After speaking with David about the worsening situation, I went back to Simon. 'Any chance of getting the deal back on again?'

'Yes, Mike is perfectly happy to do it.'

I spoke to Mike again and he was still prepared to offer the same premium on the current, much lower, share price. I insisted to David that we had to take it. But yet again, he refused.

'David, we are in dead trouble. We have *got* to take the offer.'

He still refused, but said I should discuss the matter at the next board meeting. David solicited the views of the other board members, but still took no action.

Around this time, I believe, Neil Gillis approached some venture capitalists with the idea of buying the company, but that failed to progress. Meanwhile, Blacks' bankers were getting very nervous and had threatened to reduce our facility further. In August, the company breached its covenants, and Blacks was given a short window by the banks in which to come up with an aggressive turnaround plan to safeguard its future.

In November 2009, matters reached breaking point for me. I resigned from Blacks and told the financial press that I had been 'banging my head against a brick wall'. I went on to say that 'The management was unwilling to take the tough action required to avoid a perilous outcome.' My statement also read: 'There was no crisis management. It was clear the pace of change was not going to be fast enough to bring success. It was too little, too late, and we were in a perilous situation.'

Following my departure, Blacks endured more pain and poor results. On 7 December 2011, the group was put up for sale. On 23 December, the directors stated that Blacks was likely to enter receivership. The company was effectively insolvent and the shares likely to be worthless. JD Sports acquired Blacks and Millets out of receivership.

The galling thing about all this was that the outdoor concept was trendy. It was a growth area, and yet, even with two established brands like Blacks and Millets, we hadn't been able to make it work. The whole experience was immensely frustrating. In hindsight, and purely from a business perspective, it was interesting to see how things could go wrong as a result of having the wrong people in the wrong places, pursuing a flawed strategy, while failing to pay attention to what was going wrong or take swift remedial action.

David Bernstein is a thoroughly decent, professional man, but, in my opinion, he is not someone you want on your team when the chips are down and strong leadership, commercial decisions and actions are the order of the day.

My experience at Blacks led me to consider the roles of various board members more generally. Strictly speaking, the chairman's role is to run the board and ensure that the non-executive board members are deployed to add value by way of expertise, experience or contacts within the industry. The chief executive is tasked with carrying out the strategy set by the board and running the company, and is also responsible for meeting or, better still, beating the budget and organising the management team in such a way as to operate efficiently, while ensuring that the right people are in the right jobs at the right time. What's more, the CEO can be mentored by the chairman, and a good working relationship between them is an important factor in ensuring that the whole management team fully understands the direction of travel and the pitfalls along the way.

Irrespective of who does what, it is vital that the board operates effectively and openly, and that each member feels they can offer a useful contribution, propose alternative strategies and reach decisions. Those decisions then need to be carefully monitored to ensure that they are having the desired effect. These checks and balances and fine-tuning can make all the difference between attaining the end goal and falling short.

Of course, in real life, these roles may be blurred or changed to accommodate specific needs or personalities. In my role as executive chairman, I always took a very hands-on approach. It was the only way I could ever be.

From eleven-a-side to five-a-side

The years leading up to the start of the new millennium, and those immediately following, had certainly been turbulent. I tend to make light of it all now, and insist that there was nothing actually wrong with me – just a lot of fuss over a hernia! I had rolled my sleeves up again, and relished being back in the rough and tumble of business.

In September 1999, I had been discussing my career options with Nat Solomon – a wonderful gentleman with a great sense of humour, a sharp mind and excellent City contacts. He was a former chairman of Tottenham Hotspur plc, but our connection with Spurs was not the only thing we had in common – he had also worked at Unilever, although we had not been contemporaries. Nat suggested I speak to someone called Patrick Dunne at 3i, the multinational venture capital firm. The company was originally established to provide long-term investment funding for small- and medium-sized businesses, but grew to become the largest provider of growth capital for unquoted companies in the UK.

I met Patrick, who offered to put me on the Register of Non-Executive Directors. In essence, this is a list of experienced industry experts or entrepreneurs who make themselves, and their experience and expertise, available by sitting on company boards and advising the other board members. These individuals do not take an active role in the day-to-day management of the business. In some instances, the non-executive's reputation in the marketplace could enhance the perceived value of the company, or give other investors confidence and comfort, but that was not at all what I was looking for. I told Patrick that I wanted to get stuck in and run a really troublesome company. I was pretty persistent and, eventually (probably just to get me off his back), he introduced me to Nick Badman, a 3i director, who later went on to be the managing director of 3i Group plc.

I liked Nick, because he was straight and to the point. He sent me off to look at a couple of companies in which 3i had made investments and which required further funding. It didn't take me long to reach my assessment. I relayed my unequivocal findings that these companies were too far gone and strongly advised against any further investment. My exact words were: 'They are still twitching, but they are dead.' That must have struck a chord with Nick – and I am pretty sure he knew the truth long before he received my report. It was just a test.

Not long after, I was invited to look at another one of 3i's problem investments – a company called Powerleague. This company specialised in hiring out 'small-sided football pitches'. I had absolutely no idea what that meant. However, from 3i's perspective, this was a marriage made in heaven! They knew I had expertise at turnarounds and, with my

Tottenham experience, I surely knew all about football. I tried to explain to 3i that professional football had only the most tenuous of links with five-a-side football, but my pro-testations fell on deaf ears. They had found their man, and 3i wanted me to go in as executive chairman and sort it out.

I think it's worth going into quite a lot of detail about Powerleague, because it's an instructive turnaround case. As a prelude to taking on this challenge, I dropped into a number of the centres and spent some time reading through the research about the scalability of the business, what sites were already in the pipeline, the availability of future locations and potential sites, and the building cost of estab-lishing a fully functioning centre. It occurred to me that this was a clever business.

Powerleague tapped into a niche and growing market of people who enjoyed playing football, but needed a new way of playing. They had commitments on the weekend and perhaps did not relish the thought of playing on a muddy pitch with only the most basic changing facilities and cold showers. They also probably struggled to get twenty-two people (eleven on each side) together in a remote location on a Saturday or Sunday morning.

The attraction of the Powerleague offer is that it can be friendly or competitive and can be played with just five play-ers on each side. The playing field, which resembles grass (but is actually synthetic), can be floodlit during the week and has adjoining it a reception area, full bar and social area, hot showers and other modern amenities – all available 364 days a year. On top of that, the pitches are easy to book and affordable, parking is free and the clubhouse is friendly and warm. The target age is eighteen to thirty-five, and, for the older age group, the convenient, casual nature of the five-a-side format allows players to extend their playing days. The facilities also had male and female changing rooms and were starting to attract a few women's teams.

Powerleague itself had come about early in 2000, through a merger of two five-a-side companies in which 3i had acquired significant shareholdings: Anchor, based in Scotland, and Powerplay, based in England. After investing around £50 million, the result of 3i's investment was some twenty sites and significant losses. Furthermore, immediately post-merger, there were more directors on the board than centres!

In order to bring some sanity and rationalisation to the company, 3i had appointed an experienced board. The chairman had come from the hospitality industry, where he had been very successful, and he brought in others from that sector.

Unfortunately, the integration of the two companies was not running smoothly: the forecast turnaround was not happening, the losses were mounting and the board were at loggerheads, with a number of directors defecting and setting up rival businesses. In the face of this, 3i were in despair and very concerned about the prospect of recovering their investment.

But when I looked at the names of the directors, I was stunned and contacted 3i to let them know that I would not be taking this opportunity forward. By a strange quirk of fate, the incumbent chairman, Stephen Poster, had been my next-door neighbour throughout my childhood. My parents had been lifelong friends with his, and Stephen, who was a couple of years older than me, used to help me with my homework. According to 3i's instructions to me, my first act would be to remove him! There was no way I was going to do that.

The following day, 3i came back to inform me that they had explained the situation to Stephen and that he was more than happy to pass on the 'poisoned chalice', and he called me to wish me luck.

The company suggested that I might want to go to Hackney Marshes over the weekend as there was a tournament taking place, advertised as 'the world's biggest five-a-side football event'. Powerleague had undertaken to run it. They created or marked out fifty pitches and somehow or other managed to juggle the three thousand teams that had entered. Fifteen thousand men between the ages of eighteen and thirty-five generated one hell of a lot of testosterone!

I was fascinated by the excitement and enthusiasm of all the players in their various team colours, and particularly noticed one fellow who appeared to be running the event virtually single-handed. He was rushing around everywhere and, somehow, had his finger on the pulse, keeping the whole logistical nightmare together right up to the grand finale on the Sunday evening. It was an impressive demonstration of organisational ability within a highly spirited and potentially volatile situation. I think he told me he was the events manager.

The following week, I met with Martyn Grealey, the managing director of Powerleague, and then Jerry Bernstein, the operations director, who were both highly critical of the management team. They had clearly identified that the key to turning around the five-a-side business was to develop the hospitality side. It was a no-brainer from their perspective. The football side was peripheral and a drain on resources. With the excellent parking facilities and live screening of Sky matches, the sports bars would be the driving force of the business.

Later that week, I went up to Glasgow and made my way to Powerleague's head office in Paisley. They were based in a quaint building on a very large site with a five-a-side football centre attached to it, but I have to say, I was underwhelmed by the fact that no one was playing football on those pitches.

I met one of the directors, Morris Payton, who struck me as quite an aggressive individual and overly keen to let me know how important he was to the business, because, amongst other duties, he negotiated all the purchases associated with the five-a-side centres. He was dismissive of Grealey, Bernstein and a number of other senior managers and suggested that I sack them and install him as managing director. I then met Jez Hall, who was the director in charge of finding and negotiating new sites. He displayed an encyclopaedic knowledge of the UK, and was very enthusiastic about how to grow the company. Finally, I was introduced to Sean Tracey, the guy I had seen running around organising the event at Hackney Marshes. He struck me as rather quiet and composed, and explained that he had been working at Anchor/Powerleague since leaving university, and had worked his way up from branch manager at Powerleague's Glasgow centre to national sales manager and new openings manager. He knew the business from the ground up.

I identified in Sean someone who understood the

potential of the business and with whom I could work. The unanimous voice from the Paisley guys was that the driving force of the business was the football, and the bars were a nice add on, in contrast to the new management team's view that the bars were the core of the business.

I already understood Sean's strengths, but Jez's role was unclear to me so he had to explain the process. His job boiled down to pretty much this: he would get into his car every morning and drive around all day looking for sites that might accommodate and be suitable for a five-a-side centre. The focus of his attention was mainly school playing fields. Jez would then arrange to meet the head teacher and begin the process of selling the idea of allowing Powerleague to transform around four acres of muddy, under-utilised school playing fields into a purpose-built, state-of-the-art, five-a-side football centre.

The great attraction for the schools was that they could have exclusive use of this fantastic facility during the week from 8.00 a.m. to 4.00 p.m. and receive a non-commercial income. Powerleague would have exclusive use of the centre every evening and weekend and during school holidays. If the head teacher grasped the opportunity, then Jez would embark on the process of gaining support from the school's board of governors and start to secure all the planning consents. Where Jez really earned his money was when the head teacher, school governors or council planners raised objections. Then he had to skilfully overcome all the obstacles, keeping the process alive and moving forward. Even when things went smoothly, there were always hurdles to overcome. It was by no means a simple process.

There was often tension, because, for example, Jez

might find a school site and begin spending money without a proper evaluation of whether the local demographic and population size justified the £2.5 million investment needed to build a new centre. Aside from a lot of time and energy being expended on lost causes – those places where it was clear from the start that permissions or planning consents would never see the light of day – there were big problems with some of the Powerleague sites.

In some instances, too much money had been expended pushing through a difficult planning process to a certain point, without then going on to complete the development. Much worse still, some sites had actually been developed, but the centres were in locations with the wrong demographics. Although Jez was good at finding sites, and relentless in going through the process with the head teachers, he was not a strong negotiator and tended to offer lots of sweeteners to the schools, which then weakened the attractiveness of the final deal. There must have been pressure to grow the business and open new centres, but Jez's job was to identify sites with potential – and not build them out unless all the criteria had been met.

In order to evaluate the situation fully before accepting the job, I asked to meet with the finance director, Adrian, but was told that he was based in London and worked from home. So, instead, I went to the Accounts Department and requested a bundle of management accounts to go through. I have always found that there is absolutely no substitute for physically being in the business environment, talking to staff, watching how they interact and generally getting a feel for the place. But reading the management accounts, strategy documents, bank statements and publicity material also provides strong pointers as to how well the company is managed and organised. In the case at hand, the signs were not good. Powerleague's accounts were appalling in my view, and I don't just mean the losses. The information was incomprehensible to me – sketchy at best – and the analysis, if you could even call it that, I felt was hopeless.

The research I did threw up conflicting information, discord, strange mixes of individuals, inadequate financial information and completely different strategic ideas among the board and senior management. In other words, just the sort of challenge I relish! I decided that I was very much up for it.

It was clear as day to me that the driver of the Powerleague business was five-a-side football and that the bar-led strategy that Martyn and Jerry had been promoting and developing was not the way forward, but both disruptive and counterproductive.

I composed my report to 3i, told them that I would become executive chairman, and laid out my thoughts in my typically forthright manner. I stated that my first act as chairman would be to relieve Martyn and Jerry of their duties. I identified Morris, Jez and Sean as the people who would lead the team going forward, and noted that I would be having a very close look at Adrian the finance director. Unless I was satisfied, he would probably be going very soon.

As per usual, 3i had a representative on the Powerleague board to keep an eye on what was happening with their investment. His name was Mike Pacitti and he was an experienced non-executive and a very helpful individual.

After my first board meeting, it was apparent, as I had thought, that Adrian the finance director was not up to the job. He was reluctant to spend the time up at the head office in Paisley that I deemed necessary, so he left. I was not too concerned, because I thought that I would recruit a new finance director in due course and needed to focus on getting to grips with the multitude of other issues that were cropping up.

But 3i and Mike Pacitti, in particular, had other ideas. They were very uncomfortable about continuing to trade without an FD in place. Without consulting me, they decided to appoint an interim finance director from an agency specialising in senior interim financial staff. When I heard what Mike had done, I was absolutely livid. I took the next flight to Glasgow with the express purpose of getting rid of this person – whoever it was. First of all, he was costing the company a fortune, because we were paying the agency a fee well in excess of the market rate. But more than that, I was not going to have a situation where my judgement was being undermined.

I printed out the management accounts produced by this interim bloke and headed for the airport. To while away the short flight, I thought I would look through the accounts, thinking that they would likely provide me with further ammunition – not that I thought I needed any to remove this person. But they were good – very good. I could not believe it. The contrast between this chap and his predecessor could not have been starker. He had identified some areas of weakness: the breakdown of costs and the performance (or lack of) of each of the centres. I was impressed, but I was still going to get rid of him!

Another problem awaited me at Glasgow. Sean met me at the airport and explained that Morris had walked out on the company. Sean suspected he would be joining a Powerleague rival: Goals, a small competitor that had been formed by Keith Rogers, who had previously run Pitz, the forerunner of Anchor/Powerleague. The news was a bit of a shock to me, and a cause for concern, because Morris knew of all the sites we were looking at and targeting. However, this bad news was tempered by Sean's assessment of the interim finance director, by telling me he was 'really good'.

I was introduced to Andrew Mallett, the man in question, and immediately warmed to him. He was an unassuming, quiet man about my age, and thoroughly professional. When we sat down to go through his numbers, he was quickly able to identify and articulate areas of strength and weakness in the operation of the company and offered some ideas of how we might go about improving things. Bloody hell, I thought, how had he managed to get to grips with the chaos so damn quickly? On top of it all, he was well liked by Sean and the Accounts Department. On the flight home that evening, my thoughts were consumed with how we could keep hold of Andrew. The agency fees were outrageous, but he was worth it!

I visited a number of other Powerleague centres over the next few weeks and got a good feel for that side of the business, what looked positive and, more importantly, those factors and practices that were obviously wrong. For example, on weekdays, staff arrived at 9.00 a.m. and sat around aimlessly until the evening as most of the bookings were from 5.00 p.m. to 11.00 p.m. Some of the centres looked tired and even neglected, and staff were confused about whether they should be concentrating on the bar or the football. Mostly, they were concentrating on neither. Of course, there were some exceptional centre managers who ran their centres with real commercial nous and dedication. Unsurprisingly, those were the ones that yielded the best returns. However, the most pleasing aspect, by a country mile, was the unbridled enthusiasm of the customers, the players – they loved five-a-side.

I used to play a lot of tennis in my younger years and would happily go off all weekend to play. By Wednesdays, I would be desperate to get back on court for my regular evening game. So I understood perfectly the adrenalin rush of engaging in a sport you had a passion for.

Over the next few board meetings, and through daily conversations with Sean and Andrew, we began to get a much clearer idea of what we needed to do and how we should prioritise our efforts. Under the previous regime, staff salaries at the centres had not been well managed and there were too many staff, poorly organised shifts and basic salaries that were too high with no performance-related pay. Motivation was low and so was footfall into a lot of the centres. These were all things I had witnessed for myself.

The Powerleague model is not dissimilar in some respects to the hotel industry. If you don't sell a room, you have a net loss of potential income that cannot be recouped. At Powerleague, if a pitch slot is not filled, then you have lost that potential income. So, Sean devised a two-week plan, whereby the staff was incentivised to ensure that every night of the week, every pitch was filled. He insisted that all centre staff put in place block bookings: if players routinely turned up on a Wednesday at 8.00 p.m., they would get a discount for booking that slot for thirteen weeks. Players could then relax in the knowledge that a pitch, or even a specific favourite pitch, would be reserved for them.

Sean would ensure that every morning, every manager and assistant manager would be on the phone, cold-calling players who had turned up the previous week, and whose contact details we were now religiously collecting, to get them to rebook. It was crucial to fill those slots every night. As the weeks went on, staff got a buzz out of not only filling slots for that night, but ensuring that the week ahead was filling up, and the week after that. Another crucial aspect of this concentration on customers was that we were creating a database of eighteen- to thirty-five-year-old males. A great target market.

Andrew was beavering away in the background, keeping control of everything and identifying centres that were lagging behind. Then Sean would visit them and establish precisely what was going wrong. If there was a training need, Sean would make sure that the staff had a thorough understanding of what was required. If staff could not cope, or were not gaining traction, they were replaced. He promoted assistant managers from within to give them a chance to work the system.

Over a relatively short period of time, we had removed the staff who had been recruited by the previous management and focused all staff on the football side of the business. We put in place a reward system based on filling the slots, and Sean started a league table of Powerleague centres to promote some friendly rivalry. That also had the desired effect. Sean was well respected, had a good rapport with the centre staff and, having worked in their positions, knew exactly what each job entailed.

Powerleague also ran leagues for the teams. These were competitive games with a qualified Football Association referee which pitched teams against one another. Once again, Sean focused the staff at the centres to contact teams and ramp up their enthusiasm to try and encourage them to play perhaps two competitive matches a week, rather than one. Social bookers were also encouraged to play one social game per week and one league match. Sean and his team further spiced up the competitive aspect of the leagues by introducing a system of promotion and relegation.

After about nine months, the green shoots of a turnaround were certainly beginning to come through. I had made it clear to Jez that we would not build another centre for twelve months. He could continue to make inroads and find any excuse to slow down those sites where we had a green light to develop and the board had agreed to do so. I wanted to get the current estate in order before we moved ahead with any further capital expenditure.

Meanwhile, Mike Pacitti, the 3i representative, was very encouraged with the progress that was being made, and must have admired the transition from a hopeless situation into one that looked promising. At the same time, however, in spring 2002, there appeared to be significant strategic changes taking place within 3i. There was a shift away from smaller investments, such as Powerleague, in favour of a concentration on very large ones. So, 3i approached me and suggested that I should turn my attention to finding a buyer. I went to great pains to tell them that if they gave me twelve months, I would turn Powerleague around and they would probably recover a good proportion of their investment.

But 3i were adamant: they did not want to wait. They had decided to write off a large proportion of their investment and said that if I could sell the company for but a fraction of the amount invested, I would share the upside fifty–fifty with them, but the condition was that they wanted a quick deal.

I think word of 3i's intentions must have got out, because I was approached by a small five-a-side operator called VIDA. It was owned by David Murray, who also owned Rangers Football Club. I had a number of meetings with VIDA, which had just seven or eight centres and were based in Edinburgh. VIDA wanted to merge with Powerleague, with VIDA taking management control and moving the head office to Edinburgh. I could not see the point of that, given that Powerleague owned the freehold of the Paisley head office and had twenty centres. Roles and responsibilities was another area that we couldn't agree on, so I walked away. I dodged a bullet on that deal, because VIDA folded a short time later.

I had more faith in pursuing my own path after this near miss, because I could see there was an opportunity here – in some ways it would have been easier to sell, but I felt that there was more value in proving that the business was good by continuing with the changes we'd started to implement.

Keith Rogers's Goals, Powerleague's competitors, also took a meeting with us around this time. Had common sense prevailed, we could have, and should have, come to a deal. However, there was a fair degree of rancour in the room. Rogers seemed to think of himself as the supremo, and was lauding it over Sean, his former employee from their Anchor days. He was accompanied by Morris Payton, who had walked out on Powerleague when we were at our most vulnerable. Goals were being funded by a venture capitalist and had installed Sir Rodney Walker as chairman. I met with them as well, and was assured that they had the funding in place to acquire Powerleague. But I didn't like them and I didn't like the deal.

I came away from the Goals meetings believing I needed to find a different solution. I decided to meet with Powerleague's bankers, Bank of Scotland, who had been supportive of the company. My plan was that they fund *me* to acquire Powerleague. After a couple of meetings, and some very tense discussions that I had with a Dutch shareholder who had a minority interest in Powerleague and initially didn't want to sell, the deal was done. Bank of Scotland took a fifteen per cent stake and bought out 3i. Meanwhile, I acquired eighty-five per cent of Powerleague.

A new dawn!

Floating Powerleague

The thing about venture capitalists, and indeed professional investors, is that there is no emotional attachment to their investment. They have funds to invest and stakeholders to satisfy and are very careful to ensure that their investments yield the required returns. Indeed, one of the key criteria before they invest is to consider the exit strategy and the timing thereof.

Notwithstanding all their due diligence and professionalism, by the very nature of investing, there is risk. Some promising companies fail to deliver the anticipated or forecast returns, and, within a certain time frame, end up not fulfilling their promise. In the case of 3i and Powerleague, I guess that 3i had become disillusioned and, where I saw opportunity, they just saw more risk.

There is no doubt that 3i made a mistake in exiting from Powerleague at this point in time. I felt strongly about this and had told them that, given time and support, they would recover a good proportion of their investment, and I had demonstrated that the direction of travel was now positive.

Apart from poor management and a flawed strategy, at the point when I bought out 3i, Powerleague was still heavily indebted following the merger of Powerplay and Anchor. Added to that, the company had gone over budget in building out a number of new sites that were in their ramp-up phases and were not yet profitable. So, the overall position was that the meagre profits were insufficient to cover the high interest payments. In effect, I was the eighty-five per cent shareholder in a company with no real shareholder value, given the debt position. Notwithstanding that, I was absolutely determined to make a success of this venture, and had a vision of how things might pan out.

I was strongly of the opinion that I could not make things happen without Sean Tracey and Andrew Mallett. Having now worked with them for nine months, I knew they were two exceptional individuals, and we worked well as a team. I offered each of them shares. To my amazement, Andrew said that he didn't want any shares because he did not see his longer-term future with Powerleague. He enjoyed the diversity and freedom of being an interim finance director. He also expressed concerns about breaching his contract with the recruitment agency that provided him with that work. I told him I would fix that, but he was immovable: he wasn't committing his future to the company. Having said that, like the honourable man that he was, he agreed to stay until a replacement was in situ.

I was dismayed, but eventually recruited Sheena Beckwith. Although she had absolutely no experience in five-a-side, she was very organised and capable and fitted in well with the team. Andrew left Powerleague after a good handover period, with the company on a much sounder footing than when he had arrived.

At that time – it was now towards the end of 2002 – Powerleague operated twenty-four large, outdoor, five-a-side centres. What we needed was to have an even greater focus on getting more people to come to our centres. Crazy as it may seem, we offered a play-for-free initiative, just to make some of the newer centres look busy and in the expectation that once the players came along, they would engage. That worked well. We placed even more emphasis on cold-calling companies and offered them deals to come and play at our centres as a teambuilding exercise. We contacted local companies and suggested they might like to play against each other; then we contacted companies in the same industry and told each one that their rivals had expressed interest in having a five-a-side competition against them. All the while our centre managers and staff were diligently collecting names and contact details, building the database and following up to encourage players to get together with friends or workmates to come along and have a game.

We were creating demand, but we also needed to fix the bars, which had few checks and balances: a delivery would arrive, but there was little or no effort to reconcile the order with what was delivered, or to monitor stock. So we initiated stock control processes and regular physical stock checks. All alcohol and soft-drink orders required head office approval, and the centres were required to check deliveries, rather than just accept that what had been ordered had been received.

In short, the management team, and indeed every single member of staff at the centres, were now focused on the core business requirements of selling the pitch slots, managing the bars properly and sprucing the places up.

However, what was required was an even greater degree of effort and experience at the centres. A number of the centre managers and assistant managers were either recent graduates, or young, keen and enthusiastic, but needed to learn the ropes. We promoted a number of the experienced managers to area managers. This proved to be a shrewd move and sales continued to increase, with a number of the newer centres picking up momentum. The area managers fed information back to Sean and, as a result, the initiatives that worked well in one centre were then trialled in others. Similarly, difficulties in one centre were fed back and solutions were found and disseminated to the other centres.

Having said that, there was no real homogeneity throughout the sites, and things that worked well in one place did not always work well in another. There was great disparity in the performance of the best sites, and those that had appeared to reach maturity, but did not enjoy the same level of performance. In some cases, it was a management issue that was relatively easy to fix; in others, it was because mistakes had been made in evaluating the potential customer base of the centres, and, for sure, a number of the centres would never reach the level originally envisaged. Also, Powerleague was beginning to experience the pressure of competition. This came in two guises: smaller, aggressive competitors, such as Goals; and, of greater concern, local councils that provided inferior facilities, but at very low prices.

At the time, we also had a one-size-fits-all approach to building the centres. This did not appear sensible to me, and I will explain how I addressed this situation, to great effect, a little later.

At head office, internal processes and procedures were implemented and very tight controls were maintained. As we now had visibility of the two-week forecasts for every centre, it was much easier to see which were filling the slots and which were failing to do so and had empty pitches at core times. Kenny Green, our IT supremo, was instrumental in bringing greater transparency and efficiency to our processes. We were also now always in a position to reconcile the cash from each centre with the amount actually banked. These measures, particularly the cash management, had very positive effects in ensuring that the cash taken at the centres was easily reconciled with the bank statements.

With all these things under tight control, the key was to fill the pitches outside the core times. Most players wanted to play between 7.00 p.m. and 9.00 p.m., Monday to Thursday, so we needed to put some further effort into the 5.00–7.00 p.m. and 9.00–11.00 p.m. slots as well as the weekends. Again we introduced incentives, with cheaper prices for those times, and we pushed hard to develop weekend leagues.

During school holidays, we attracted a lot of younger five-a-side enthusiasts, and encouraged soccer schools to use our facilities. These youngsters, after all, could be our future customers. We promoted birthday and football parties at our centres and that also worked well. A number of professional football clubs also began using our centres for training, and this provided us with a further opportunity to promote and market ourselves to the local community.

In centres that were located near universities, we were

able to fill slots during non-core periods, but naturally at deeply discounted (i.e. student!) prices. Nevertheless, it all added to the sum of the parts.

As time went by, and the performance of the great majority of the estate improved, we came to realise that we needed to begin a programme of refurbishment. A number of the older, more established and busy centres looked tired and a bit run down. What was also apparent was that technology had moved on and the pitch surfaces at our astroturf centres were no longer 'best of breed'.

A new artificial grass carpet had become available and formed part of the new centre specification. This so-called '3G' surface was being used by Goals and we recognised that we needed to upgrade a number of our prime sites with it, too.

The refurbishment programme was hugely successful and improved the look and playability of the pitches. Every centre we refurbished saw significant increases in turnover and customer satisfaction. We took the opportunity to increase our prices, and found no resistance to this. Over time, we continued to move up the price points at centres where we were reaching hundred per cent occupancy, or had no local competition.

We also had to get a little stricter with players who booked pitches and then failed to turn up, because this inevitably led to a loss of pitch income. In an effort to eliminate the loss of income from no shows, we took credit card details from telephone bookers and made it clear to them, and to block bookers, that we would charge their credit card even if they failed to turn up. Clearly we did not want to appear to be too draconian and the centre managers applied common sense and allowed some latitude in genuine cases, more often than not taking the payment but giving the players a credit to play on another occasion.

All these measures and many others continued to improve the performance of the estate. I derived a lot of pleasure from meddling in the centres closest to me – egging on the managers of the Barnet and Mill Hill branches to outperform first each other and then the most successful Scottish centres. The business started to thrive on this kind of friendly rivalry and I felt that the employees' pride in their branch was an important component of our ongoing success.

Sponsorship deals provided another new source of revenue soon after the refurbishment programme. In conjunction with the 2002 World Cup, Powerleague held a major national event, sponsored by Budweiser. The success of this event led me to believe that we could attract a number of other sponsors. Clearly, the level of income that could be derived was not in the same league as those negotiated during my time as CEO of Tottenham Hotspur; however, I was sure that pitch branding would be of interest and we would be able to secure some lucrative sponsorship deals.

I was still a non-executive director of Blacks at the time, so I approached the board and suggested that our sportswear fascia First Sport might wish to have some branding at Powerleague centres, particularly where the centres were close to the First Sport stores. This worked well and gave us the impetus to go to other companies and test the market appetite for this kind of association.

Sean led this initiative and it proved to be very successful. Indeed, Xbox became our first major sponsor, as they correctly identified that our target market of eighteen- to thirty-five-year-olds was a perfect match for their video games consoles. Being linked with Microsoft, the developers of Xbox, gave Powerleague a very good profile, and led us to explore and achieve a number of other lucrative sponsorships deals. I recalled that Lucozade were very keen sponsors of football clubs, so they joined the growing list of top brands and companies with whom we entered into sponsorship deals. Some time later, Lucozade became our 'headline' sponsor. In this way, although five-a-side was very different from the professional game, my Tottenham experience did end up contributing to successes at Powerleague. Perhaps 3i's original assessment of me had been correct!

We were paying down our debt and making the interest payments, but what I really needed to do next was to kickstart the programme of growing the company. For that, we needed additional cash to build a number of the sites that Jez Hall had identified and been keeping warm.

We secured further funding from Bank of Scotland, who had been supportive throughout and were very pleased with the excellent progress the company was making. That money paved the way for a cautious expansion programme. Having understood the needs of our customers, it was imperative to provide the best possible facilities for them. We needed great pitches and playing surfaces. The reception area, clubhouse and changing rooms needed to be serviceable, and easy parking was essential. The key for me was to meet these criteria, but at a much cheaper price than we had traditionally budgeted for.

I came up with the idea of a modular build to address this

issue. This would be an inexpensive and flexible method of reducing the build and fit-out costs of the clubhouse, without in any way compromising the customer experience and joy of playing on excellent pitches. It also gave us the flexibility of building smaller sites with fewer pitches and a smaller module clubhouse.

It was critically important to ensure that future sites stood the very best chance of succeeding, so we identified the following criteria for appraising whether to invest in a new location:

1. A population of core customers within half an hour of the site. This translated roughly into a player base of around 3,500 to 4,000 players. Sean's preferred measure was a population of around 200,000 people less than ten minutes' drive time away.
2. Good local road network and accessibility, a key determinant of the catchment area.
3. The level of active football within the catchment area. Generally, where the site was close to a football club or traditional football pitches, we could predict there would be an interest in Powerleague.
4. Good-sized local businesses as a means of accessing potential *groups* of players rather than having to target individuals.
5. Competition within the catchment area, although this criterion could be viewed as a double-edged sword. On the one hand, it meant that there was an established population playing five-a-side. On the other hand, the centre might be hampered when trying to sell slots on either side of the core time

(what we called 'shoulder time' – 5.00–7.00 p.m. and 9.00–11.00 p.m.).

6. How keen the school/head teacher and board of governors were to entertain a Powerleague centre on their doorstep. We always sought to ensure that the local council or community were not opposed, as this would just delay the project and significantly add to the cost.

Watford, Cardiff and Basingstoke were the first modular builds and they all proved to be successful. Best of all, the build cost was in the region of £1.25–1.5 million, rather than the £2–2.5 million that had been previously spent. We had found a winning formula.

By 2004, Powerleague was riding high. All the centres were performing in line with or exceeding expectations, and we had a good pipeline of well-qualified sites to develop. Furthermore, I had been in discussion with a number of house-builders to explore the option of disposing of a couple of centres where we owned the freehold, or had very long leaseholds, so that we could realise the cash immediately.

One of the wonderful features of Powerleague was that once the investment had been made in the centre, most of the cash generated from pitch slot sales, bar revenue and sponsorship income, went straight to the bottom line. Powerleague had become highly cash generative, but in order to accelerate the development of the pipeline and gain first-mover advantage in new locations, we needed to consider how we could fund this. The bank had been supportive of the refurbishment programme, but we needed investment rather than loan facilities for this kind of expansion.

Goals, our competitor, had recently completed a successful float on the London Stock Exchange Alternative Investment Market (AIM). AIM allows small- and medium-sized companies to raise equity to support their growth, and we gave serious consideration to this option as an alternative to further bank funding and probably a slower rate of growth.

Sean and I couldn't agree on how to develop. My position was clear. I was not in favour of a float, because I thought we were in a good situation: the company made a good profit and there was plenty of cash coming in − and I liked the fact that the management team had control of their destiny, with eight-five per cent of the equity and a very supportive bank. Sean put forward a different view, and felt strongly that an AIM float would be a better way forward. Personally, it would put him and his family in a secure financial position and professionally, it would enable Powerleague to grow quickly, taking advantage of the excellent pipeline of sites and further raising the public profile of the company, which would, in turn, give us greater access to prime sites.

In addition to my professional concerns, I had personal reasons for not wanting the pressure of the float. My father was in very poor health and I already had enough on my plate with other directorships. In the end, I conceded and we began the arduous process of preparing for the float. A network of advisors needed to be engaged so we ran beauty parades to decide which advisors to go with. If you've never been involved in an AIM flotation, then it might surprise you to know just how time-consuming it is, and how many people are involved. Here are some of them:

- The **nominated advisor** (NOMAD) provides the essential service of ensuring that the company complies with the regulatory process and co-ordinates and oversees the preparation of the AIM admission document.

- The **broker** is there to introduce you to potential investors and advise on the pricing of the shares (based on the level of interest from the investor community), can act as market-maker to ensure the liquidity of the shares and can provide an efficient means of buying and selling the shares.

- **Reporting accountants** review and report on the financial position and health of the company, and provide additional independent assurances to investors that the appropriate due diligence has taken place.

- The **law firm** conducts the legal due diligence, advises on drafting the admission document and all other legal aspects, including director responsibility and corporate governance.

- The **public relations firm** helps to craft the company story and strategy, and works with the other advisors to prepare the presentations for the institutional roadshow, which forms the basis of the face-to-face meetings with the institutional investors and maintains media interest.

I must say, I was very satisfied that in every respect, we chose excellent advisors to work with and guide us. I am still in contact with a number of the principals. Having said that, these experts did not come cheap! And not just in financial terms: we had to devote a significant amount of time to selecting them, working with them and then going on the roadshow, which involved innumerable presentations to potential investors in order to explain our business and overcome objections. By the end of it Sean, Sheena and I were not only word perfect, but we had the answer to every question and like actors, performed for each audience with the same enthusiasm and gusto.

Powerleague plc floated on AIM on 25 May 2005 with a market capitalisation of £55 million. I was absolutely delighted when Andrew Mallett and Simon Bentley accepted my invitations to join the board. In the aftermath of the flotation, I rather cheekily stated to the *Financial Times* that, with 70,000 players a week at Powerleague centres, five-a-side had become more popular than the eleven-a-side game, and also that the company's market capitalisation was bigger than those of many Premier League clubs – Aston Villa, for example, at that time was valued at £37 million. The whole point of the flotation, though, was to strengthen our balance sheet and support our expansion through acquisition and organic growth.

Powerleague's turnover was up by seventeen per cent and profit up by nineteen per cent the following year. During the year, we had managed to expand our estate to thirty-four centres across the UK. We continued our partnership with Xbox and introduced Lucozade, Budweiser, Nike and Braun, and managed national corporate events with Sainsbury's, JD Wetherspoon and John Lewis. We also trialled an affordable gym offering in a number of centres to utilise some dead space, and – an absolute no-brainer – added pitches to centres at, or approaching, hundred per cent capacity where we had spare land to build on.

Much the same story followed in 2007, with sponsorship and events revenue increasing by forty-one per cent. In addition to the extension of our modular build, we developed sites in the heart of the City of London, near Liverpool Street Station. These centres attracted a huge influx of 'City boys' who played at lunchtime and in the evening and weren't sensitive to the relatively high prices we charged for the pitches.

Clearly Powerleague was on a roll, and Goals was also growing at a rapid pace. However, one of the problems of being a publicly quoted company is the expectation that sales, profits and dividends will continue to rise. We felt under some pressure to grow at a pace that we were not particularly comfortable with. I would have been content to pause for breath, take time to re-evaluate the estate and refrain from building out any more sites. However, that option would not have gone down well with the City, and our share price might have suffered. We were on a bandwagon, and needed to meet the expectations of the shareholders and brokers who were sending out positive growth and buy signals to the market.

At the start of 2008, I received a call from Tom Knight, who had been one of my co-directors at Blacks Leisure. He was now chief executive at JJB Sports plc, the large sportswear retailer that had developed indoor five-a-side football centres next to their out-of-town retail stores. Indeed, they were now the third-largest five-a-side operators behind Powerleague and Goals. He offered to sell Powerleague their business.

We felt compelled to make the acquisition for a number of reasons. The first was that the opportunity to acquire such a significant competitor was just too good to miss. The second was that all the JJB centres were indoors and that offered Powerleague a very interesting alternative to our outdoor centres. The third was that the locations of the JJB centres were highly complementary to our existing portfolio and included the Manchester Centre, the largest five-a-side football centre in the world, with nineteen indoor and four outdoor pitches. However, what preyed on our minds more than anything else was the thought that if we did not acquire these centres, Goals surely would. That would seriously depress our share price and make Goals the top five-a-side player. Foolish, I know, but I could not allow that! We paid £17.4 million in cash from our existing resources and increased our bank facilities on the back of the acquisition.

We now had forty-three centres, and were far and away the largest operator in the market. We attracted the attention of Patron Capital Partners, who paid £23 million to acquire a proportion of my shares and become twenty-nine per cent shareholders in Powerleague plc.

Over the course of the next twelve months, Powerleague continued to prosper, in spite of the global financial crisis and stock market crash. We had always claimed that Powerleague was recession-proof, and, whilst our growth slowed, our numbers were still buoyant. However, our share price fell, and Patron took the opportunity to make a bid for the remaining seventy-one per cent of the company. The premium I negotiated hard for was forty per cent above the share price immediately prior to the moment they made their offer.

I had known for certain when Patron acquired twenty-nine per cent of Powerleague that it was only a matter of time before they launched a bid for the whole company and took it private – only the timing was in doubt. I recommended the offer to shareholders and was required to stay on for six months as part of the deal.

*

How did I feel about it? I think I took it in my stride, and reasoned that all good things must come to an end. I had done exceptionally well financially out of Powerleague and was very proud of having been at the forefront of developing what had been a basket-case company in a cottage industry into a highly profitable and well-established leader within the flourishing five-a-side market.

The fiasco at ASCO

Life is full of surprises. Towards the end of December 2003, I received an urgent call from Bank of Scotland that would challenge my ability to navigate very stormy corporate seas. I didn't know it at the time, but that phone call triggered the most ambitious and successful turnaround in my career. The challenge ahead was probably the most complex I have ever undertaken. You may find this quite a different chapter compared with the others, but I will try to show what made this phase in my life also one of the most interesting.

What was so important that it could not wait until the New Year? The answer was ASCO plc. Now, that will probably mean as little to you as it did to me in 2003. ASCO is a leading international oil services company, and, at the time, one of the largest private companies in the UK in terms of sales (about $1.5 billion annually) – just ahead of Harrods in the ranking!

ASCO's customers were the major global oil companies that required a broad range of offshore and onshore oil and gas field services to support their businesses, such as fuel and lubricant supply, logistics, warehousing, inventory and materials management, fuel transport, freight management, environmental waste disposal, tank cleaning and specialist personnel. ASCO provided all these services from its bases in Aberdeen, Peterhead, Great Yarmouth and Stavanger, Norway, typically on long-term contracts.

Still confused as to what that had to do with me? So was I.

Without going into too much of the history of the company, 3i Group had become involved with ASCO in 1996, via a management buy-in, and owned sixty per cent of the group (another thirty per cent was owned by Wood Group, a major oil and gas services company). The objective of 3i had been to grow ASCO rapidly via a programme of acquisitions, using the very strong foothold, excellent reputation and expertise gained in the UK market, predominantly in the North Sea.

A string of acquisitions took place in the late 1990s and early 2000s, particularly in the Americas. In 1998, 3i acquired L&L, a New Orleans-based company, which operated as a dockside supplier in the Gulf of Mexico, and in 2000 Venture Transport, a Houston-based transportation company. Shortly afterwards, ASCO took over the BP supply base in Trinidad and Tobago. Further expansion took place in Canada in 2002, and a subsidiary called Brasco was also established in Niteroi, Brazil.

There had been great enthusiasm for these acquisitions, because it was felt that ASCO's considerable expertise gained in the North Sea would be adopted by the companies in the US, and both knowledge transfer and economies of scale would be quickly achieved. The ultimate goal of 3i was to float a highly successful, integrated oil service logistics company on the New York Stock Exchange, and realise a significant multiple on its original investment. On the face of it, given the wealth of ASCO's expertise and experience, and its long-term contracts with all the major oil companies, this might have appeared to be a sound strategy.

Unfortunately, the acquisitions had been made at the top of the market, and soon problems started to pile up. Perhaps there had been too much optimism about the opportunities to then commit to enhancing the performance of the acquisitions. Maybe insufficient attention had been given to competition, market volatility and risk analysis, coupled with an overexuberance to do the deals. Most likely there had been too much focus on the top line (sales), and too little concern about the bottom line (profit). Finally, there was resistance – and that is putting it mildly – to the Scottish management imposing themselves on the 'good old boys' in Texas and New Orleans! It was clear that no outsider was going to tell them how to run things in their back yard, the Gulf of Mexico.

ASCO was not the first to run into these kinds of problems. Many leading companies over the years have ventured into the US marketplace with high hopes of replicating their success in the home market, only to find that they were chasing fool's gold, and subsequently retreated nursing painful losses and deep disillusionment. As I was to find out, dealing with the Americans is not the same as negotiating with the Brits, and by that, I do not in any way mean to cast aspersions or generalise, but the common language does mask a different culture and way of doing business.

A period of excitement soon gave way to a crisis, and, at the start of 2003, Colin Manderson, chief executive for six years and mastermind of the expansion, resigned. A new, experienced management team was brought in, led by Tony Powell, who had spent twenty-eight years with Schlumberger, the oil services giant, and his sidekick, Bill Graham, as finance director.

The financial demands of the business meant that by October 2003 the shareholders had decided that they could no longer continue funding the business and had pretty much dumped the problem onto the banks.

Bank of Scotland and Royal Bank of Scotland, ASCO's principal lenders, were in a bit of a bind, to say the least, and needed to address the situation immediately – if not sooner! For their part, the banks were not keen to continue funding the company either. They had little confidence in the new management team, their strategy and ASCO's worsening trading position. The company would be fatally damaged if funds were not put in place, as an imminent breach of its facility was at hand.

It's worth just pausing here to comment on the importance of the statutory accounts. At the end of that turbulent year, ASCO's *2002* statutory accounts had still not been signed or filed. These are vital for investors and lending organisations because they underpin the company's trading position, that it is creditworthy and that it has the support of the banks. If accounts are not filed in timely fashion, this creates tension and contracts may be lost or credit limits reduced or withdrawn. Late filing also carries a fine. The reason ASCO's accounts had not been signed and filed was that they needed the banks to confirm that they would continue to support the company for the next twelve months, and send a comfort letter to that effect to the auditors.

The US companies used different banks – one of which was Fleet, which is part of Bank of America. However, the businesses there were in a similarly precarious situation. They could not continue trading beyond Christmas, because they were not complying with their covenants, and Fleet had claimed that one of the US subsidiaries had included certain ineligible debtors in order to assert that banking agreements were being met.

And that, in a nutshell, was why Bank of Scotland made the urgent phone call to me in December 2003.

I met with the banks and they then sent over a lot of background material about the company, which I studied over the Christmas and New Year period. I was absolutely up for the challenge, and the banks rejected suggestions from ASCO board members to consider other candidates. The banks weren't long-term investors – they just wanted to recover as much of their £50 million debt as possible.

My very first act as executive chairman of ASCO plc was to phone Andrew Mallett, the interim finance director 3i had installed at Powerleague. He was undoubtedly one of the smartest and most hard-working people I'd ever worked with.

'What are you doing, Andrew?'

'Oh, just shopping in PC World.'

'No, I don't mean right now. I mean what are you doing workwise?'

'I'm the interim FD for an awful company. It manufactures ovens. I hate it.'

'Good to hear! I have the chance of a lifetime for you. You missed out big time on Powerleague, so don't miss out on this chance. I need you to join me. I want you to be deputy chairman, and I will split my shareholding fifty-fifty with you.'

'Oh, Claude, I don't think so.'

'Andrew, please think about this. I am starting on the fifth of January. Come to Aberdeen with me.'

'But I have made a commitment to the oven company.'

'You'll have to renege on that commitment, Andrew. Really, you'll have to. I need you. You come, Andrew. When you see the challenge, you won't leave. I guarantee it.'

It must have been a difficult time for Tony Powell and Bill Graham and their new management team. They had been in situ less than a year, but they had not been quick enough off the mark. Perhaps they had underestimated the problems that they would encounter, and relied on expensive consultants to look at global opportunities and determine how to deal with the issues, thereby wasting money and losing time. They had clearly misjudged the scale of the task and the shareholders' willingness to throw good money after bad.

Initially, I was keen for them to stay on for a while and help me to get the company into some shape. Tony was helpful, but didn't like the fact that I didn't consult with him: I just took a proactive stance to resolve situations and short-circuited the normal formalities. Within a few weeks, they both decided to hand in their notices. I released them from their obligations to give twelve months' notice and, within a month, they were gone. Indeed, the situation was so precarious that a number of the non-executive directors also resigned.

I recall the first item on the agenda for the first board meeting I chaired in the New Year was health and safety. I thought it was a joke – the company was in imminent danger of imploding! – but the board member reporting on the issue went to great lengths to explain where the exits were in case of an evacuation of the building. However, it was a great reminder to me that the most important thing about an oil and gas company is its safety record. ASCO was rightly proud of this and took every care to ensure that all its processes and procedures were designed, at all costs, to avoid any injury to its employees or personnel on any of its sites. Companies such as BP were obsessive about safety and awarded important contracts to ASCO on the basis that their safety procedures were best in class.

Having said that, I couldn't wait for the board member to finish so I could start addressing the urgent problems. I received reports from the directors and discussed possible solutions to try and resolve some of the most pressing issues. The most important short-term problem was getting the banks to provide some emergency funding to the UK and US businesses in order to continue trading and to provide the necessary comfort for the auditors to file the accounts.

The plan that Tony and Bill had been working on to achieve this was to dispose of the US companies and exit the US market. The shareholders had recognised that the acquisitions had been a very expensive mistake and their investment had by and large been lost. The acquisition foray had been poorly negotiated and executed, and had impacted badly on the core UK business. A number of the companies had already been put up for sale, a process being managed by the corporate finance specialists Simmons & Co., based in Houston. However, either there had been no interest or the tentatively offered amounts had been derisory, as none of them had been sold. In the end, I took a very active role in getting results.

The oil industry is highly cyclical and sensitive to the oil price, and one of the many problems at the time was that that the industry was in a downward trend in the cycle. This translated into a drop in exploration activity and the cancellation of drilling programmes. The direct knock-on effect was a lower level of fuel required for the vessels servicing the offshore rigs. ASCO in the UK had entered into a number of long-term charters of platform supply vessels and each of these was costing around £10,000 per day. This low level of activity meant that the vessels supplying the rigs with fuel, water and equipment were often idle.

I made contact with the vessel owners and pleaded with them to take their vessels back and allow us to walk away from the contracts. They refused. Great efforts were made to enter into short-term contracts to enable the company to recover some of the costs. Fortunately, within a few months, activity picked up and the vessels were all working again and earning the company around £15,000 per day.

At the same time, our competitors were taking advantage of rumours in the market of ASCO's difficulties and attacking our share of the customer base in the UK. Nevertheless, the long-term relationships, our excellent and enviable safety record, and overall performance over a number of years meant that our customers did not desert us. This stability in the UK market was not matched by that of our principal companies in the United States, however. The performance there was both disturbing and woeful.

My particular bugbear at the time was Venture Transport – the company ASCO had acquired in 2000 – which was proving difficult to sell. It was based in Houston, Texas, and the president of the company was a man called Ronnie Murphy. He was, in fact, also president of the ASCO holding company in the US, which meant that he was in charge of all of the US companies. Venture was a high-volume and low-margin ground transport business, specialising in the energy industry. In essence, it contracted with over a thousand owner–operator tanker drivers, and to encourage these owner drivers to work for it, the company took on their vehicle insurance.

The problem was that the number of accidents incurred, and insurance claims made against Venture, had become so considerable that its insurance company had imposed an excess per accident of $350,000, and then would delay or refuse to pay very large claims. Meanwhile, Venture was also being sued by accident victims and their families. We were inundated with claims and legal fees and I could not see a way to resolve the situation such that would induce someone to buy Venture. All the transport companies that were approached by Simmons took one look at the situation and passed on the opportunity. My only option was to try and persuade Ronnie Murphy himself or a consortium led by him, to acquire Venture.

The Houston head office, where Ronnie was based, was a magnificent building that had formerly been a bank and was expensively and lavishly furnished and equipped. Ronnie was obviously very proud of his hunting prowess as his office was adorned with the stuffed heads of many of the animals he had shot. He also had numerous photos of himself shooting with his buddy, President Bush Senior.

Although Venture was losing money and had a huge

overhang of problems, Ronnie did not appear to be too bothered by anything and certainly had no appetite to curb company expenditure or sack anyone. I've spoken to employees who were there prior to my arrival who had the following to say: 'The directors were having a great time on the company expenses: luxurious apartments, limos, private jets, first-class travel, dinners and evening entertainment at strip clubs was common practice and bragged about openly. It was not unusual to have all the group MDs flying to the US for meetings, which cost the company hundreds and thousands of pounds. Clients like BP were challenging these costs hard; they felt that clearly ASCO was making too much profit on their contract if they could afford these extravagant lifestyles.'

I saw some of this extravagance at first hand. On one occasion I decided to drive to one of the other companies in the Houston area and asked if a car could be rented for me.

'You don't need to do that. Take one of the pool cars.' They had a number of cars that were leased and just sitting around.

Worse was to come. After a long day at the L&L head office in New Orleans, I decided it was time to head back to the hotel. One of the managers turned to me and said, 'Why don't you stay at the company apartment? You'd be more comfortable there. Ronnie always uses it when he is here.' I later discovered there were two more luxury company apartments in Houston, used by previous management when they were in town.

Naturally, I gave instructions to terminate the leases on all the apartments and pool cars. In the scheme of things, and given the problems and issues facing the companies in the US, these were merely gestures, but they sent out a message that we needed to batten down the hatches.

After many meetings and months of gentle persuasion, and hours of sitting with Ronnie and trying to avoid returning the gaze of the dead animal heads staring at me, I was pretty sure I had reached an agreement with him to buy Venture Transport. He decided to take the weekend off to come to a final decision. I hung around all weekend and on Monday was keen to finalise the deal. Ronnie's PA informed me that he was 'stressed' and had decided to take a few days off at a 'retreat'! He eventually returned on Thursday, fully refreshed, and, together with a new business partner, completed the purchase.

Within a week of my appointment as chairman of ASCO, I had received an unsolicited approach from a private equity investment company specialising in the oil and gas sector that wanted to acquire ASCO's UK business. The indicative offer was, in my view, derisory and I had no hesitation in rejecting it, on the basis that once the banks had provided further funding and Andrew and I had had a chance to evaluate the problems and get going on resolving some of the issues, we would surely be adding value and be in a better position to assess the worth of the business.

Some six months later, the same investors revisited the situation and made an improved indicative offer of around £35 million. By that time, Andrew and I had really got stuck into ASCO and had a good appreciation of the strengths and weaknesses of the UK business. In fact, ASCO in the UK was a very good company indeed, but it was being held back by a number of issues: some onerous contracts (including the vessel charters I have talked about), a deficit in the pension scheme, a disastrous waste management contract in Glasgow and some significant under-investment in plant, to name but a few. Having discussed the new offer with Andrew, the banks and the board, I rejected it as it did not come close to representing the true value of the company and also undervalued the potential of the group.

Andrew and I continued to make real headway in resolving issues, and worked closely with a core of senior managers, who were riding out the storm and contributing to winning key contracts, and retaining those that were coming up for renewal. Andrew's work ethic was beyond admirable – I might call his line in the UK office to leave a message for him at 6:00 p.m. US time and he would pick up the phone. I found out later that it was not unusual for him to work through the night in his dedication to resolving the pressing issues.

Our efforts were noticed by the banks. In May 2005, Bank of Scotland and Royal Bank of Scotland wrote to me: 'As I expressed at our meeting in London on 19 May, both BoS and RBS wish to stress their satisfaction with the performance of yourself and Andrew Mallett during your stewardship of ASCO. We recognise that your achievements have been considerable, especially in the light of the extreme difficulties faced by the Group at the time of your arrival.'

In spite of the UK banks' complimentary words, this was not a marriage made in heaven, and there were a number of occasions when I would scream at Alan Ferguson, my nemesis at Royal Bank of Scotland, mainly because of the bank's absolute refusal to provide further funding for the US subsidiaries.

Further discussions took place with the UK banks, which in February 2006 decided that it might be opportune to see if ASCO UK could be sold. Included in the deal would also be some of the smaller subsidiaries in Canada, Mexico and Trinidad, as well as an excellent freight forwarding company in Houston. Jeffery Corray, the managing partner of KPMG Corporate Finance, Aberdeen, was tasked with managing the sale.

KPMG spent a considerable amount of time with Andrew in compiling the detailed information memorandum and preparing the management presentations, business plan and financial model to be sent out to interested parties. Then KPMG assembled a list of potential purchasers and those eligible parties with the interest and financial means to make the acquisition.

A number of interested parties emerged: a few trade buyers, predominantly competitors, and some financial private equity groups. After numerous discussions, all managed by Jeff Corray and his team, it boiled down to two private equity players, both of whom seemed determined to make the acquisition. The bidding began and was nerve-wracking. Jeff, in his calm and measured way, ran the process as each of the buyers bid up the price. At £90 million, things began to get very interesting. Jeff was very pleased that there was tension and kept both players dangling, excited and believing they would win the prize. When we reached £110 million, I was beginning to lose my nerve, and at £115 million, I urged Jeff to call it a day and accept. He kept his cool and told me that he sensed that there was another round to go before he believed he had reached the high point. At £120 million, I *pleaded* with him to accept. In October 2006, Phoenix Equity Partners acquired ASCO UK for £125 million.

It was a thrill and a pleasure working with Jeff, and although KPMG earned a princely sum for completing the transaction, which included a number of ratchets once the price went above the £100 million mark, they were worth it!

All the bank loans were repaid in full, plus a lot more, and there was still further value to be extracted from all the non-UK-based companies in the portfolio. It was an occasion for Andrew and me to celebrate, as we were significant financial beneficiaries as a result of the transaction. (As a postscript to this, at the end of 2011, Phoenix sold ASCO on for some £250 million to Doughty Hanson, and the company has continued to thrive.)

*

I have already outlined some of the problems and the relaxed attitude displayed by the senior management at Venture transport, the US company ASCO had acquired in 2000, and which we successfully sold to its president, Ronnie Murphy. However, a very different set of problems presented themselves at L&L, the fuel and lubes business that the 3i Group had acquired back in 1998.

The L&L business should have been relatively straight-forward. On the fuel side of things, the company purchased diesel from the major oil company refineries in Louisiana and Texas in 1.2-million-gallon loads, which were then delivered by means of company-owned barges to all the company docks located on the coast of the Gulf of Mexico and the banks of the Mississippi river. The diesel was then discharged into our huge overground tanks for storage and sold on to vessels that were en route to the offshore oil rigs in the Gulf of Mexico. Another important part of the business was disposing of the waste product that these vessels brought back from the rigs. It was a complex and hazardous operation.

The lubricants operation involved picking up product in bulk with tanker trucks and delivering it to the docks for resale. The key to this business was to buy product at the lowest possible market price and then sell at a higher price. Whereas the buying price is set daily via the Platts Index (a kind of commodities exchange which sets a benchmark price), the selling price is determined by the competition. L&L had eighteen excellent dock locations.

Port Fourchon, Louisiana's southernmost port complex, was home to many oil service companies. Its docks serviced ninety per cent of the Gulf of Mexico's deepwater production. There were six hundred oil platforms within a forty-mile radius and they produced eighteen per cent of the US oil supply. L&L had two prime locations at Fourchon, but on numerous occasions could not take advantage of those key positions because its lack of cashflow hampered its ability to purchase enough diesel. This situation was compounded by the major oil companies, which exploited L&L's weak financial situation by forcing a change in the trading terms, from settlement in three days to payment in advance. Very often, Danny Brown, the president of L&L, increased his prices at the docks to artificially high prices to deter buyers, as he had little or no diesel to sell.

Misery was piled on misfortune when Hurricanes Katrina and Rita devastated New Orleans in the summer and autumn of 2005, turning it into what looked like a war zone, with windows shattered in the main city, vacant office blocks plunged into darkness and absolute carnage in low-lying areas, where people were robbed of their homes and possessions, not to mention some lives. Some of L&L's docks were seriously damaged and business came to a standstill, causing yet more problems.

L&L was also in a mess as a result of an ill-fated contract that ASCO had entered into with BP. A new dock in Port Fourchon called 'Magnolia' was commissioned and building commenced, but, partway through, the funding from the UK ceased and L&L was forced to complete the project using bank finance that was specifically earmarked for working capital, not building a new facility. This brought about a fearsome reaction from Fleet, ASCO's US bankers, who cried foul and threatened to put L&L into Chapter 11, a form of bankruptcy protection in the US. This would have destroyed the credibility of the company. I had some very heated exchanges with the Fleet bankers who I felt were being unreasonable and unhelpful. They insisted on putting in a quasi-administrator in to monitor the situation, and, in spite of my protestations, they prevailed. I saw this as a prelude to them instigating their threat of Chapter 11.

During this very fraught period, I met the president of one of L&L's competitors, Gary Chouest. We got on well and Gary agreed to acquire the Magnolia dock for $12 million. I remember him suggesting we do the deal on Monday and asking me if I wanted to fly my plane over to his place or did I want him to 'swing by' and pick me up in his plane. I opted for the latter!

A solution was in sight, but just before we were due to finalise the deal, I phoned Gary to confirm the details of the meeting. He told me that he had changed his mind and had decided to fly to Florida and play golf. With that, he put the phone down on me! A few days later he phoned me and offered to buy Magnolia for $7 million, rather than the original $12 million. He was toying with me. I told him he would never acquire Magnolia and I would never do business with him and put the receiver down. In the end, I concluded a deal with Todd Hornbeck of Hornbeck Offshore, which provided L&L with a cash injection and enabled us to continue operating from the base. In the long term, it was a better deal than the one envisaged with Gary.

Meanwhile, even though I had disposed of part of the problem, Fleet were piling the pressure on L&L and made further threats to put the company in Chapter 11. I mustered my forces and explained the precarious situation to the UK banks. I have to say that they were tremendous on this occasion. The very next day, their representatives were on a plane with me to New Orleans to confront Fleet and the quasi-administrator. We obtained a 'stay of execution order' from Fleet. Fleet gave L&L one more month to find another bank to fund it, and left me in no doubt that in thirty days Fleet would certainly put L&L in Chapter 11. They took pleasure in telling me and Danny Brown, L&L's president, that we would never get refinanced.

Those thirty days were absolutely manic. Andrew and the accountants John Coutrado and Mike Hartsell at L&L put together an excellent business plan and forecast, and contacts were made with local and national banks. We had numerous conversations with banks, but no one was that keen. Finally, we received a call from Wells Fargo. They appeared interested and wanted to meet the management team.

The L&L management team were decent people, and Danny was a really genuine, hard-working and knowledgeable guy. He had worked his way up and knew his business inside out, which was just as well, because I spent hours and hours in the office discussing L&L's fortunes – or, more often, *misfortunes*!

In view of the arrival the next day of Wells Fargo's representatives, I instructed John and Mike, the accountants, to come to the office smartly dressed in order to create the right impression with the prospective new bankers. That's all very well, but the weather in New Orleans is hot and sticky. Everywhere is air conditioned, of course, and apart from Danny and his team, the L&L head office was not frequented by people from outside the company. The dress code was therefore 'relaxed', to say the least.

Andrew and I arrived for the meeting in our suits, naturally, but I was beyond dismayed to see John and Mike in jeans and grubby-looking T-shirts.

'Guys, I told you to smarten up for Wells Fargo.'

'Yes, this *is* our smart gear.'

Andrew and I looked at each other and shook our heads in despair and proceeded to do a dry run through the presentation. Finally the Wells Fargo team arrived – a cheerful lot all dressed in … jeans and grubby T-shirts! Andrew and I looked decidedly out of place.

Instead of getting down to business, Danny told them some jokes that I didn't understand, offered them coffee in plastic cups and some doughnuts and they chatted about the New Orleans Saints (American football, apparently). It was as though they were old buddies who had popped in for a coffee and donut and a bit of a chat. I was mystified and very worried. Eventually, the L&L team went through their presentation, and it went really well. Wells Fargo liked Danny, they liked the company, and they even liked the two funny English guys in suits.

A couple of days later, they came back and were enthusiastic about taking over from Fleet as the company's bankers. Danny had the greatest pleasure in telling Fleet that L&L had indeed found new backers, and Andrew and I never wore suits to L&L again.

Having disposed of the Magnolia dock problem and resolved the banking situation, Danny and his team were now in a position to get back to running the business. The numbers improved and profitability was restored, albeit not to the levels experienced prior to the ASCO acquisition. In 2008 and 2009, L&L prospered and managed its business well. There were no breaches of bank covenants and sales were quite buoyant, with margins and profits in line with expectations and a programme of much-needed capital expenditure initiated.

Then, in early 2009, the UK banks became rather keen for me to get the ball rolling to dispose of L&L. We had a number of approaches, but either the offer was derisory or the party making the offer could not raise the funding to make the purchase.

The banks, in effect, just wanted to get rid of L&L and were keen for me not to push the exit price too much, but I was loath to do that for a number of reasons. First, it is not in my nature to just sell, regardless of the price; second, I wanted Danny and the management team to have a say in who acquired them. Danny had always been aware that the end game for the banks was to dispose of L&L, but I felt a duty to make sure that the acquiring company looked after them properly. Finally, Andrew and I pledged some of our incentive bonus to Danny and his team. We wanted them to do well out of the transaction and, above all, work with us to make it happen.

Then, as you might remember, on 20 April 2010, the Deepwater Horizon rig that was chartered to BP suffered an explosion that sent oil gushing out into the sea for eighty-seven days. The Gulf of Mexico was devastated, with some 200 million gallons of oil discharged during the period. The environmental impact of the disaster is being felt to this day.

L&L's activity in the area came to an immediate halt. There was no possibility of doing any business whatsoever as the Gulf of Mexico was shut down. As a result of the explosion, President Obama imposed a six-month moratorium on deepwater drilling in the Gulf of Mexico because of concerns about the safety of oil and gas exploration. The docks too were contaminated. Naturally, L&L made insurance claims and via our excellent US lawyer, Scott Willis of Correro Fishman Haygood, we set out multiple claims against BP.

You can imagine that the oil crisis didn't make it easy to sell off L&L, but in August 2010 I was approached by Rubin Martin, the president and CEO of Martin Midstream, a much larger competitor, who expressed a strong interest in acquiring the company. Danny was very satisfied that Rubin would be the ideal partner, both in terms of his excellent fit with L&L and good personal rapport. We got on well and very quickly agreed a price. Rubin stated that he required absolutely minimal due diligence as he was very familiar with L&L's operation and could close the deal quickly.

Naturally, once the lawyers and accountants got involved, the due diligence process was somewhat more extensive than Rubin had made out, but we had already provided information to previous suitors and it was easy to set up the data room and provide Martin Midstream whatever further documentation was required.

I was in regular contact with Rubin while all this was going on, and we agreed that we should keep that channel open in the event of anything untoward cropping up. The process was not completed within the agreed ninety-day exclusive period, but I was comfortable that real progress was being made and no issues of substance were arising. My only stipulation in granting him a further exclusive due diligence period was that I would not accept any reduction in the agreed purchase price under any circumstances.

On 31 December 2010, Martin Midstream acquired L&L. At the closing, L&L's claims against BP had not yet been settled, so I proposed to Rubin that Martin Midstream pursue the claim on the basis that we would split the claim settlement fifty–fifty. As is absolutely normal in these transactions, a proportion of the selling price, in this case several million dollars, was held by our lawyers in escrow for twelve months, pending any claims against L&L or any tax issues that might arise.

We had been transparent with Martin and certainly did not anticipate any claim on the escrow, and indeed none was made until 31 December 2011! Yes, exactly a year later, just as the period in which Martin could claim was about to expire, our lawyers received an utterly, outrageously absurd letter stating that we had misrepresented a host of matters and that Martin had been pressurised into completing the transaction before they had undertaken full due diligence.

For the next eighteen months, our lawyers received an absolute barrage of letters from Martin's lawyers, asserting more and more ludicrous and unsubstantiated violations allegedly perpetrated by L&L, and our lawyers responded to each one by categorically denying any wrongdoing. Martin's spurious claim grew and grew, and eventually reached $11 million. Their lawyer even declared in August 2013 that this was the twenty-sixth official exchange of correspondence.

In the middle of all this, in 2012, Andrew told me that he had prostate cancer, and by early 2014, his condition had become much worse. He was dying. He asked me to do him a favour and settle the matter with Martin. It had been causing him some anxiety, and he wanted it off his mind. I phoned Rubin that afternoon and after some initially frosty exchanges, I settled the matter via a full and final settlement of $700,000 dollars. The escrow money was released.

Andrew passed away on 2 December 2014. He was a great business partner and a true friend. I miss him a lot.

The claim that L&L had made against BP in 2010 took a very long time to be settled. John Coutrado, the accountant, had evaluated the loss at around $12 million and a deal had been struck for our lawyers to work on contingency and share in the settlement from BP. The lawyers were very confident of a significant payout, and were emboldened when, in September 2014, BP were found guilty of gross negligence and wilful misconduct under the Clean Water Act. They were fined some $20 billion by the US government, and in total paid out $63 billion for clean-up, restoration and compensation.

Never in my wildest dreams (or nightmares) did I imagine that, some thirteen years after accepting the job at ASCO, I would still be involved in finishing off the mandate. On 11 March 2016, I received an email from our lawyers to advise me that the federal district judge had dismissed our moratorium claim against BP, along with hundreds of others. The judge had bizarrely determined that the moratoria, and not the oil spill, had been the cause of the losses, thereby granting BP's motion to dismiss the moratoria claims. On 12 May, the lawyers wrote to advise me that mediators had negotiated a settlement figure of just $1 million in respect of the L&L claim, and both BP and Martin had accepted the settlement. The last chapter of ASCO's ill-fated US adventure had been closed.

*

The stress at the time was huge, but looking back, ASCO was the most exciting business I have been involved in. The knife-edge negotiations and brinkmanship required to keep the company going across continents and cultures, and the myriad different characters I had to deal with to bring about a successful turnaround, are times I remember with pleasure and a great deal of satisfaction – at least from the comfort of 2016!

The Apprentice – the interviews

Last year, my wife Thelma and I went on a holiday to Vietnam. We were very keen to visit all the sites and learn more about the country's troubled and war-torn history.

I had never been to the country, even though I was a US citizen and could have been called to serve my country in the Vietnam War. I vividly recall going to the US Embassy in London in 1968, just as the Americans were in the depths of fighting in Vietnam. I was nineteen at the time and assessed as medically fit and available for military duty, but in the end I was not drafted.

It was absolutely frightening to learn of the carnage caused by the American bombings and the way in which the Viet Cong enticed the US troops into all sorts of horrific, primitive and highly effective traps. The Viet Cong soldiers were unbelievably resourceful and built tunnels in which they hid and lived for extended periods. It was at once terrifying and mind-blowing.

Although I am claustrophobic, I decided that I wanted to go into the Cu Chi tunnels, an immense network of deep, dark tunnels and caverns that you can just about crawl along. As I was about to enter the tunnel, a voice in an Australian accent shouted out: 'Claude! Is that you matey?' I looked around to see a complete stranger, in the middle of nowhere, calling out to me ... An *Apprentice* fan! He had seen me some years back when *The Apprentice* had aired in Australia and could not resist the opportunity to become acquainted and get a selfie. Our potentially meaningful friendship was abruptly curtailed as I hurriedly descended into the tunnel.

I mention this as a preamble to my story of *The Apprentice*, to demonstrate the reach and influence of factual entertainment TV shows, and especially those as successful as *The Apprentice*. I have featured in the UK version of the show since the very first series, aired way back in 2005. At the time of writing, I have just finished filming series twelve. Before you ask – no, I won't be revealing the winner! But I can certainly fill you in and answer some of the questions I am frequently asked about the programme, and give you the inside track on what really goes on.

As usual, though, I am getting ahead of myself, and need to set this out in two stages. The first revolves around my role of interviewer, which I have held right from the start, and the second involves my newer role as 'the eyes and ears' of Lord Sugar.

*

As you must have realised, I have a very hands-on management style, and, in 2004, I was immersed in the fiasco at ASCO, as well as the pressure of Powerleague's turnaround. I had maintained contact with Alan Sugar and his family throughout, and we would always get together for a bit of a chat when attending the Spurs' home fixtures. It might have been at that time, or via other mutual friends, that I learned of Alan's keen interest in becoming the star of the UK version of *The Apprentice*. I was familiar with the US version and found it hugely entertaining. I was not party to, nor aware of, who else was being considered for the part, and had had no thought or interest in getting involved. One thing I was sure of, though, was that if Alan landed the role, he would make it a success.

News subsequently filtered out that Alan had indeed been chosen as the star, and he had picked Nick Hewer and Margaret Mountford as his sidekicks. Nick and Margaret must have been obvious choices because of their close association with Alan over many years – Nick on the PR side and Margaret on the legal side. I had also had dealings with Margaret and her firm Herbert Smith when I was at Spurs. Her reputation as a brilliant lawyer had preceded her, but I had discovered to my consternation that she is also someone you don't mess with. When I first instructed her, I boldly stated that I didn't expect to be charged for her work. She replied in no uncertain terms that I was not Alan Sugar, and Spurs would be charged at full rate!

Not long after landing the starring role, Alan approached me about *The Apprentice* and informed me that the penultimate episode of the show would involve the candidates undergoing a rigorous interview. He wanted me to conduct them. I probably asked a few questions to satisfy myself that what was being asked of me was within my area of competence, and quickly agreed. It was a new, and challenging, business-related programme and I had really liked the US version.

As my involvement was limited to one episode, I just

arrived on the day of the interviews, having received the CVs of the final four candidates only a few days earlier. I think it is worth emphasising that the only information I had concerning the candidates was their personal statements and CVs. We never had any sight of the process they would be going through, or any rushes of the tasks, nor did Alan ever seek to influence me or the other interviewers in any way. We were each given free rein to conduct the interviews in any way we chose.

For my first interview, I was positioned in a tiny room on Alan's top-floor suite at Amstrad's head office. I interviewed Tim Campbell, Saira Khan, James Max and Paul Torrisi. I ran the interviews in a serious manner, was very courteous and polite, and listened carefully to the answers, following up with further questions. A single cameraman was positioned behind me, shooting over my shoulder. At the end of each interview, the camera was moved to shoot from behind the candidate's shoulder, and I was instructed to say nothing – and just nod!

The other two people interviewing the candidates were Paul Kemsley and Bordan Tkachuk. I had known Paul for a number of years as he was, at that time, vice chairman of Spurs, so we met at all the home games. I knew Bordan less well, but had heard of him over the years as he had been in charge of Amstrad Australia and was the chief executive of Viglen. We conducted the interviews one by one, using a rota system. Once we had all interviewed the candidates, we were invited back to Alan's house, where we sat around his kitchen table and discussed them, giving Alan our assessment of each candidate over a cup of tea. I will tell you that I was in favour of James Max to go through to the final.

That was all I knew until the programme was aired on

BBC Two in February 2005. I was absolutely enthralled with every episode. It was absolutely brilliant, and Paul Torrisi was a laugh a minute! What a character. Of course, the star of the show was Alan – who could have doubted that? He was brutally honest, tough, sharp and on top form. It was dawning on me that the programme had legs, and I was a part of it!

I couldn't wait for the interview episode, and my family all turned up to watch me in action. Well, quite honestly, if you blinked you missed me! My family just loved teasing me about my 'failure to launch'. My cause was not helped by the fact that my first-choice candidate, James Max, got fired and didn't make it to the final. Tim Campbell eventually became the worthy winner.

For series two, I was a bit more clued up and had begun to realise that, whilst the interview was a key rite of passage for the candidates and crucial to the final decision that Alan would make in terms of hiring, there was no need for me to be quite so polite or formal with the interviewees.

Paul Kemsley was a natural, a big character in real life who produced moments of TV gold. Bordan was also excellent. He settled into his role as the person who calmly and effectively dismantled candidates who claimed to have admired Alan Sugar from the moment of their birth, but, when challenged to answer a fairly straightforward question about the man or Amstrad, failed dismally. These type of exposures made for brilliant TV and were also instructive about the risks of telling porkies on your CV – something many of us may have done (or been tempted to do) at one time or another.

The Apprentice was certainly gaining traction and, apart from some very entertaining candidates, all the 'talent' – as we were referred to by the BBC – were playing their parts in making all the episodes compelling and hugely entertaining viewing.

Quite by chance, I was handed an opportunity to say what I was thinking during Paul Tulip's interview. He struck me as overconfident and I thought I glimpsed a look of fear in his eyes. As I went through his CV, he boastfully commented, 'Everyone likes me. I get on with everyone.' Quick as a flash, I countered, 'Well, you're not getting on with me.' He visibly slumped in his chair and, at that moment, I knew I had scored a potentially fatal blow.

I emerged from the interview room with a feeling of achievement, but when I revealed to Alan my delight at having brought Tulip down a peg, he snarled, 'Why did

Surely they can't be talking about me?

you do that to Paul Tulip? I rated him and now I can't put him through!' My winning goal had unwittingly become an own goal! Fortunately, both Paul and Bordan also rated Tulip unfavourably, so my exchange with him was one of the soundbites that made it past the edit and onto the screen. In a very small way, I had arrived.

The Apprentice moved from BBC Two to BBC One as the audiences grew, and the show became ever more popular with viewers, television entertainment pages and commentators. I became established in my ruthless interview role, and, whilst *The Apprentice* had introduced me as 'Sir Alan's global troubleshooter', the press had marked me very differently. They cast me as a villain, with comments like 'Claude Littner, the kind of man who makes your typical Bond villain look like Wayne Sleep'. Others described my interviewing style as 'lethal', and dubbed me 'a character assassin' and 'a Rottweiler'. Worse was still to come!

In series five, the standout candidate I interviewed was Yasmina Siadatan. Unlike other candidates I had interviewed over the years, she was already in business with her brother, apparently running a successful restaurant. It occurred to me that it might be useful to have some additional information about her, so I secured her company's statutory accounts which are in the public domain. I held them in reserve, in the event that the interview happened to dwell on any significant elements that might involve scrutinising them.

In the interview, it didn't take long for Yasmina to let me know how successful her restaurant business was, and how much profit her company was generating. I queried her profit figure, unsure if the number she had given was gross profit, net profit, or something in between. She stumbled badly and grew very flustered. She did not know her numbers. She could not express the difference between gross and net profit. She could not even tell me what the word 'turnover' meant.

At this point, I pulled out her accounts to check the turnover and profit figures she had claimed, and the blood visibly drained from her face. Her expression was one of surprise, shock and horror. 'Have you got my accounts?' she mumbled.

'Yes, I do,' I calmly replied.

'How did you get those?' she asked.

'They are public documents.'

'Oh,' came her deflated reply.

I inflicted more pain by stating that it was a sad indictment of her that she did not know her own company's figures, and dismissed her. Without doubt, it was a very uncomfortable experience for Yasmina – but great TV!

Another hapless candidate that year was James McQuillan. He walked into my interview room and my instant impression was that of a very nervous, awkward and vulnerable individual. He had good reason to be worried, because his CV was perfect ... for me! I lured James into a false sense of security by telling him that his CV was 'exceptional'. He quietly replied with 'Thank you', to which I immediately retorted, with a slightly raised voice: 'Exceptionally bad, that is.' He was crestfallen!

One of the questions asked of all candidates on their application form is 'Why do you want to be Sir Alan's next apprentice?' James had responded: 'Because I can bring ignorance to the table.' I scornfully read this line out loud in the interview, and James dug his own grave by arguing, 'It's a good style of ignorance.' I told him not to be daft, and, on another point, called him a prat.

As it turned out, in spite of her unfortunate interview experience with me, Yasmina went on to win that year, landing the £100,000 job in one of Alan's companies.

*

I can understand why candidates might be tempted to make some outrageous statements on their application forms in order to be considered as a candidate for *The Apprentice*. It is simply a way to distinguish themselves from the thousands and thousands who apply every year. Fair enough. However, when confronted with these ludicrous comments, it's advisable not to try and justify them. Best to 'fess up', tell the truth, make light of the claim and try to move the interviewer on to a more productive area of your achievements.

On the other hand, sometimes sticking to your guns can also impress me. In 2010, *The Apprentice* was into its sixth series, when, amongst others, I interviewed Stuart Baggs. Even today, some six years later, that interview is still recalled vividly by *Apprentice* fans, who can recite it to me, word for word. It has had hundreds of thousands of hits on YouTube. What I've never spoken about before is my perspective on how the interview progressed.

Supposedly, at just thirteen, Stuart had launched his own telecoms company, which became a limited company when he reached eighteen. He was twenty-one when he became a candidate on *The Apprentice*. His CV was full of self-aggrandisement. He had the temerity to refer to himself on his CV as 'Stuart Baggs, The Brand'.

The interview started well for me when Stuart stretched out his hand. I rudely ignored it because it was important to unsettle him from the outset. I'd stamped my authority on the interview by declining that one small gesture. I went on to read aloud to him from his CV: 'I'm Stuart Baggs, the Brand'. 'What on earth are you talking about? You're a twenty-one-year-old kid. You're not a brand.'

Stuart: 'I think, when you look at what a brand means . . . '

I jumped in because Stuart was taking control. I cut him short, telling him in no uncertain terms: 'Don't tell me what a brand means! You're not a brand. *You* are not a brand.' Inside I was seething that this 'boy' had dared to challenge me.

Stuart calmly and thoughtfully put me in my place: 'I think I might be.'

I needed to move on; Stuart had slightly taken the wind out of my sails with his sheer bravado. I challenged him by asking why someone as successful and innovative as him, someone as big a dreamer and – yes, I said it sarcastically – such a *brand*, would want a job with Lord Sugar. I now had him on the ropes and had re-established my authority as the interviewer.

'Because, at the minute, I'm a big fish in a small pond.'

'You're not a big fish. You're not even a *fish*.' Game over. He wasn't going to recover from that.

Stuart was a memorable character and candidate, one who will stay in my memory as an entertaining and larger-than-life character for many years to come. And so it was with great sadness that I discovered that on 30 July 2015, Stuart was found dead in his apartment in Douglas, Isle of Man. He was just twenty-seven years old.

For anybody who thinks that any part of *The Apprentice* is scripted, I hope that my conversation with Stuart shows how it absolutely can't be. Just as well, because otherwise you wouldn't get moments like that. Naturally, in a real-life interview situation, the whole point is an exchange of information – not an exercise in control and one-upmanship.

By total contrast, I vividly recall Joanna Riley's interview that same year. Joanna was a cleaner who had started her own cleaning company in the Leicestershire area with a number of lucrative contracts under her belt. However, she had low self-esteem, thinking that she was 'just a cleaner'. I explained that what she had was a cleaning company business, and she was growing the enterprise in an area in which she had expertise. That was the important factor. Unlike Stuart, though, she lacked confidence and self-belief, and definitely didn't think of herself as a brand!

The interviews had very quickly become one of the highlights of the series. In fact, another 2010 candidate, Paloma Vivanco, who had been fired in the episode just preceding the interviews, introduced herself to me later at the 'You're hired' screening, to say how sad she was to have been fired in episode ten, because she had so been looking forward to being interviewed by me! And she wasn't the only one to express their disappointment over the years at missing out on that interview.

In series seven, the format of the programme had changed, and instead of a £100,000 salary and a job at one of Lord

Sugar's companies, the prize for the winner became £250,000, and a '50:50 business partnership with Lord Sugar'. I thought that that was an absolutely fantastic innovation in the development of *The Apprentice* format. For me, in particular, this represented a new challenge and one that I absolutely knew I could do and would enjoy. Candidates still had to prepare a personal statement and CV, but, in addition, they also needed to provide a business plan outlining, in some detail, the new business start-up that they wished to embark on with Lord Sugar if they won. The candidates' business plans are locked away and returned to those candidates who are fired prior to the interview stage, without being scrutinised by us.

The candidate who sticks firmly in my mind from the first year of the new format is Tom Pellereau. An amiable and polite man, he described himself as an inventor. His business plan ran to some one hundred pages of incomprehensive gobbledygook, with complex drawings of a unique office chair that Tom had designed for people with bad backs. Honestly, it was at the extreme range of absurd, and commercially made no sense whatsoever.

In the interview, out of pure desperation, I asked Tom if he had any other inventions that were a bit more straightforward. With a sense of unbridled excitement, his spectacles almost steaming up, he described an innovative nail file that he had apparently invented, which filled a gap in the market and could be manufactured cheaply. It sounded a lot more interesting than the 'electric chair', but, to my dismay, when I asked him why he hadn't chosen that product for his business plan, he said he thought the office chair was the better idea. Alan must have been intrigued by the nail file idea, though, because Tom eventually won *The Apprentice* that year, and has since gone on to develop a successful business from that invention.

In series eight, there were again a number of fascinating business plans to scrutinise. I really enjoyed the intellectual challenge of reading through and analysing the plans, and spent an inordinate amount of time reviewing and researching until satisfied that I understood every detail, number and projection. Since many of the plans were in areas of business in which I had no prior knowledge, I spent time on the internet investigating the relevant industries and trends. By the time I came to interview 'the final five', as they became known, I knew the candidates' business plans back to front.

Ricky Martin was unlikely to get beyond the interview stage, based on his description of himself in the personal statement – 'The reflection of perfection' – and the fact that he likened himself to 'the god Thor'. He was a professional wrestler and I was looking forward to metaphorically launching at Ricky with a body blow that he'd be unlikely to recover from.

In the interview, I called his personal statement 'crass, obnoxious and infantile', and believe me, it was. However, when I came to review his CV, his achievements *were* highly commendable. He had a degree in biochemistry from Cardiff University, and, importantly, had, for some years, been successfully working for a recruitment agency specialising in the biomedical field. It was, therefore, with some sense of delight that I read his very well-written business plan outlining his intention to set up a recruitment agency for the pharmaceutical industry. He would be specialising in an area

The Apprentice - the interviews

of business in which he already had expertise, in a field in which he was well qualified. The key for me, then, was to strip out all the bravado and idiotic personal statements to find out what he was really like.

Ricky was good – very good. When talking about his proposed business, he was intelligent, articulate and focused. In fact, I was mesmerised. Here was a young man with knowledge, confidence and commercial acumen. I knew Alan would see that as well.

The other strong candidate that year was Tom Gearing, who ran a fine-wine investment company. Alan had a difficult choice, but came down in favour of Ricky. It is worth pointing out that he is a really good bloke, and, unsurprisingly, is now running a very successful recruitment company in partnership with Lord Sugar.

In series nine, the standout candidate, for all the wrong reasons, was Jordan Poulton. I remember getting really annoyed at his demeanour and, more than that, the fact that he was presenting a business plan in which he was not a shareholder while cutting Alan's shareholding down to a meagre fifteen per cent. That was most definitely not the deal. Over and above all that, he was depriving a more worthy candidate of the chance of reaching the interview stage. I called him a parasite and, after some further choice words, dismissed him from the interview.

Neil Clough was also in the final five in series nine, but his concept for an estate agency was, in my view, a nonstarter. In the same way as I had encouraged Tom Pellereau to come up with a plan B, I offered Neil the opportunity of adapting his proposal, but he remained absolutely adamant that his plan was a sound one. Alan came up with the classic comment before firing him: 'Right man. Wrong plan.'

Leah Totton was blessed with beauty and brains! She was also a very fast talker, and during the interview I had to ask her several times to slow down. Dr Leah's business plan was ambitious for sure, but I did not doubt her ability to make a success of it. Alan must have agreed, because she won and became his business partner. In keeping with the previous *Apprentice* partners, Leah has made a success of her cosmetic skin clinics. She has also strongly indicated that I would benefit from some of her treatments!

Apprentice fans will have been stunned and amused in series ten, when Solomon Akhtar headed for the window instead of the lift because he was so befuddled and discom-bobulated after I ejected him from his interview with me. As the interview was on the 43rd floor of a City of London tower block, that exit would not have proved a soft land-ing. Solly had an excellent CV and had started a business whilst at university, but when it came to the business plan, he just produced eight pages of pictures of sailboats. I was very irritated:

'It's a bloody disgrace. A bloody disgrace.'

When he tried to argue the point, I stopped him: 'You're taking the piss. Please leave.'

Solomon was a decent young man with an impressive CV, but you don't go into the interview episode with a business plan full of pictures!

And here is an important point: if you are starting a business and do not require third-party funding, then you don't have to prepare a formal business plan. However, if you *do* require an outside investor or funder, it is imperative that you go through the process of writing a business plan that clearly summarises your proposal and details the way in which you will develop the business. You will need to cover the funding requirements, the market, the competition, the projected profit and loss account, the balance sheet and the cashflow schedules. Pictures of sailboats won't cut it!

Another of the final five whose business plan did make an impression on me, was Roisin Hogan. An accountant and clearly very bright, her idea was based on a ready-meal format lifestyle product, using the konjac plant as the main ingredient to produce a low-calorie, carbohydrate-free, noodle food. Roisin was absolutely confident that her products would readily find their way into the major supermarkets, but I was not convinced and questioned the health aspect, amongst other issues. Getting national distribution in the major supermarkets is very tough, with well-established global brands spending vast sums on advertising and promotions, and the supermarkets' own brands occupying premium shelf space.

Roisin's numbers, although comprehensive, as you might expect, were just too wildly optimistic – a real hockey-stick graph – and I just could not see how a £250,000 investment would be anywhere near enough to break into the market. I strongly suggested that she might want to dial down the forecasts and propose a more modest growth trajectory, but Roisin was adamant and would not budge from her plan.

I enjoyed Bianca Miller's business plan, not only since it was expertly presented by a very credible candidate, but also because the subject matter was a new range of 'nude' hosiery designed to suit all skin tones. I told you before that being exposed to business plans in all different industries is very educational, and you'll be pleased to hear that I am now a bit of an expert on hosiery!

The winner in series ten, however, was Mark Wright. Confident and engaging during the interview, his business plan was in an area in which he had already had a lot of success and experience: digital marketing. Increasingly, candidates' business plans have been focused on using social media – an area that sometimes challenges my old-fashioned ways of understanding and doing business.

*

I have conducted countless interviews, both on and off screen, and people often ask how I assess the CVs. At the base level, I look for gaps and inconsistencies, becoming suspicious if there are any unexplained periods. I am incredulous when a fairly junior individual claims to have completed a multi-million-pound deal, when in reality he was, at best, part of a team, or more likely the bag carrier. In short, I like a well-presented document with a positive outlook and honest content.

The covering letter to the target company should indicate that the applicant has a genuine interest in, and some knowledge of, the company, and that his qualifications and experience are a good fit for the advertised job.

Having said all that, nothing beats the interview itself, and, if you are in a position to be granted an interview, it is imperative that you get it right. Arriving on time is essential, as is dressing appropriately. Make eye contact and give a firm handshake, whilst taking your cue from the interviewer as to how formal the proceedings will be. Answers to questions must not be monosyllabic, but, by the same token, not overly long and monotonous. It is important to be yourself, but on a really good day.

If asked at the end of the interview if you have any questions, do not ask how many days holiday you are entitled to, but try and pick up on an interesting point from the interview, or, better still, have a question already prepared. Finally, you need to leave the interviewer in no doubt that this is the job opportunity you really want, and are more than capable of fulfilling.

Of course, the tough character that has evolved over the years on *The Apprentice* is not at all what I am like in the real workplace. Or so I thought! It came as a bit of a shock when some former work colleagues ventured to tell me that, actually, it *was* very much what I'm like, and that watching me on TV brought back uncomfortable memories!

The eyes and ears of Alan Sugar

The air around me was high with the smell of fresh fish as I surveyed the scene: Billingsgate Fish Market, 4.00 a.m. on a brisk May morning in 2015. I had conflicted feelings. On one hand, I was distressed about jumping in a car at 3.00 a.m. in the morning to head to the East End of London; on the other, I had never been to the market before and it was absolutely fascinating.

I was on a balcony overlooking the market floor and was mesmerised: the intense activity, shouts and gestures of the traders; the extraordinary numbers of gleaming, fresh fish laid out ready for sale; and then the building itself – a beautiful Victorian structure that had seen so much change. It was exhilarating, despite the antisocial hours, and marked the start of a dramatic change to my public profile.

Some months before the tenth series of *The Apprentice* was aired, Alan mentioned to me, in confidence, that this would be Nick Hewer's last year as his advisor. Nick had been there from the start, but his other interests, such as the television series *Countdown*, were making it impossible for him to commit to the next series.

Some time later, Alan asked me to pop into his office. He asked if I might be interested in taking over from Nick to become the other advisor alongside Karren Brady. My immediate reaction was 'no'. I regarded the on-screen advisor roles as undemanding and unchallenging. I, like so many millions, had only seen the fully edited programme, and didn't appreciate what the role really involved. I was not interested, but very happy to continue doing the interviews, the part that I really enjoyed.

Alan said, 'Look, don't give me your answer now.' (I thought I just had!) 'Have a look at these videos of the previous series' boardroom scenes and get back to me. I have to warn you that if you do take up the opportunity, it will be very hard work.'

I watched all the videos, which were unabridged versions of what we all see on TV. I began to understand a little more about what the role really entailed. Nick and Karren really were Alan's 'eyes and ears', because they knew exactly what happened on each task. Their input into the programme was absolutely critical. I got a better impression of the detailed questions asked by Alan, as well as the comments made by Nick and Karren. The role began to look more interesting than I had first thought. In spite of this, I still had my doubts.

When I returned the videos to Alan, he suggested that, as I was still uncertain, I would do well to have a word with Boundless, the production company that makes *The Apprentice* for the BBC. He said they would be able to provide further insight into what was involved. I already knew them, so went along to chat with the managing director, Patrick Holland, the executive producer, Cate Hall, and the series editor, Francesca Maudslay. I then also met with Jo Wallace, the executive producer for the BBC. They were all super people and very encouraging and excited by the prospect of my taking on the new role. They were unanimous in their opinion that my breadth of business experience, coupled with my close association with Alan, would be perfect, and would add a new dimension to the show. Indeed, as part of the evolution of the programme, the role of advisor could be enhanced to encompass more instructive business comments to camera whilst the candidates were performing tasks. They all agreed that I would be 'amazing'.

I then met with Karren, whom I had known for some years, and who had been one of the interviewers in the early series before taking over from Margaret Mountford in series six as Lord Sugar's advisor. Karren gave me further details about what the job really entailed, and ended with a warning that confirmed Alan's earlier words: it was really exhausting work.

Once I thought I understood what was involved, I decided that I would indeed like to do it, with the proviso that I could continue with the interviews. Alan seemed pleased, if only because I had finally made a decision! My appointment, however, was kept completely under wraps.

As you know, if you have watched the programme, each series of *The Apprentice* begins with an initial meeting between Lord Sugar, his advisors and all the candidates (we call it Boardroom Zero). What you may not be aware of, however, is that this is preceded by many months of behind-the-scenes work by business consultants and Boundless, the production company, analysing and selecting the candidates from the tens of thousands of applications received.

Furthermore, the tasks themselves have to be very carefully devised and thought through. Alan is very much at the heart of the task development. He is involved in the early brainstorms, consulted on their development and has the final sign-off on them. Business messages are at the core of every task, and Alan's wealth of business experience plays a big part in what makes each one so successful. There is no end of organising to ensure that the projects are actually feasible within the allotted time scale, and that all variables are considered within the multitude of scenarios that might develop during the teams' quest to win the given task.

For example, on the cross-Channel discount buying episode in series eleven, the candidates were tasked with buying a range of items, a number of which were relatively obscure. They had to determine not only which location in northern France might stock the items, but also which of these goods might be more easily found in Kent. It was therefore imperative to ensure, prior to the filming, that these items would be on sale in the relevant areas during the period in which the task would take place. To ensure that the tasks are possible to complete within the allotted timeframe, dry runs of some tasks are undertaken. It's this kind of attention to detail that is imperative to ensure that the competition is fair.

Feasibility is by no means the only issue: each task has to be legally viable. Licences for just about every scenario imaginable have to be put in place, for instance, if the apprentices want to set up a market stall and start selling something. All these matters require prior approval from the council or local trade organisations. So multiple scenarios covering most possible events are set up, so that the candidates have as much freedom of choice as possible. Even permits for parking spaces for the crew and candidates' vans need to be obtained. In short, it is a logistical nightmare, but, with the way the production team operates, it becomes a marvel of organisation and efficiency.

Aside from the gruelling weeks of 5.00 a.m. starts and fourteen-hour (or more) days, six or seven days a week (and the occasional all-nighter!), there are many wonderful perks to the advisor role. The view at Billingsgate, for example, was just one of many spectacular backdrops that accompanied the tasks. In addition to impressive scenery, and the chance to visit places you wouldn't normally have access to, you meet wonderful, interesting, passionate people in the companies whom the candidates pitch to, and witness the candidates themselves developing – sometimes blossoming – under the television lights and 24/7 cameras.

But back to Boardroom Zero. This was the exciting part, when Alan, Karren and I set eyes on the candidates in the flesh for the first time – and it was especially exciting for me, in series eleven, to have a different perspective of things from this side of the boardroom. Some weeks earlier, each of us had received the candidates' CVs and personal statements, in addition to brief outlines of their business proposals.

The announcement about Nick's 'retirement' had been made, but no one knew who was taking over. So, while Alan and Karren took their places, I waited in the wings. After a build-up of tension, in which Alan pointed out to

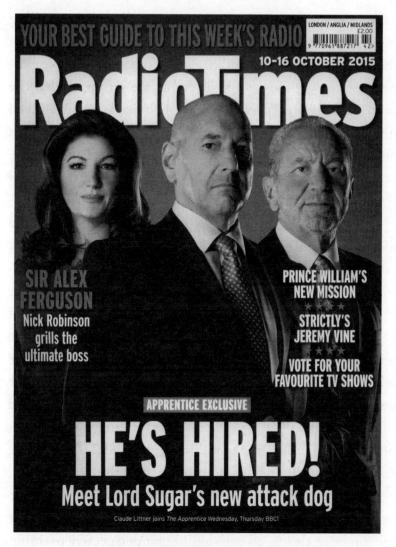

It was an incredible honour to be on the
front cover of *RadioTimes*.

the candidates the empty chair next to him, I made my
entrance, glared at the candidates, and quietly took my seat.
I had absolutely no nerves, but that could not be said of
the apprentices, judging by the expressions of surprise and
despair on some of their faces.

I noticed that Alan had all the CVs neatly sorted in piles and was fascinated to see that he had coded, marked up and made copious notes against each of them, using different-colour marker pens to highlight areas of specific interest. Clearly, he had spent considerable time scrutinising them. And to think that, throughout all those years, I had been under the misapprehension that I was the only one! I shouldn't have been surprised, though, because Alan is very neat, logical and organised in everything he does and says. Nevertheless, after all the years of being involved with him, it came as a further interesting feature about someone I thought I knew pretty well.

Before uttering a word, Alan coolly surveyed the candidates. Then, after a few moments, he kicked off by telling one of them (Dan Callaghan) to take his hands out of his pockets, which shook them up a bit more. Alan then spoke to each one in turn and made some light-hearted comments, based on what they had written in their personal statements and CVs. He teased one of the candidates, Joseph Valente, calling him Valentino. Joseph took the joke and smiled, but I noted a hint of something serious behind that smile. Perhaps he was a contender?

The purpose of this initial encounter was to give the candidates a gentle introduction to the boardroom, Karren, me, and the process in general. They were also issued with clear instructions to remain respectful to members of the public and all the other people they engage with on the task, and always to comply with instructions they were given. Alan told the candidates in no uncertain terms what he was looking for in terms of business growth from his next business partner.

He went on to let them know that he had arranged a beautiful house for them to live in whilst they were part of the process. The teams were mixed up, so that, unusually, it was not boys versus girls for the initial task. Karren and I followed the teams to the candidates' house – I was now on duty for the first time, observing. I went into the room where the team I had been assigned to observe had assembled. Here they were instructed to choose a project manager, as well as a name for their team, for the task ahead.

I was astounded at how long it took for the team to come up with a name and a project manager; they bickered and shouted over each other and, for some considerable time, got nowhere. From my point of view, the name was far less important than deciding how they were going to tackle the first challenge! My first impression of these individuals as business partners for Alan was not favourable.

Here again, I can draw parallels between *The Apprentice* and the world of work. This was a new situation and they were all overeager to make an impression and establish themselves in the 'pecking order'. A calm thoughtfulness would have been a better stance, I thought.

By the time I left the house, it was late evening and I was a bit tired, but my work was not yet done, because Alan needed to be updated on a very regular basis about exactly what the candidates had said and done. The way it works is that Karren and I copy each other into all our emails to Alan, sharing our observations and thoughts about the individual performances of the candidates. This way, the three of us are always 'au fait' with how things are progressing.

In this first instance, the points of discussion were who

chose the team name, how it came about, what other names were considered, who stood back, and who came forward. We'd also look at who became the project manager, how that came about, and who said what and how. This all seemed a bit irrelevant to me at the time, but I went along with it and emailed over the information.

That night, I was keen to get to sleep because a car was picking me up at 3.00 a.m. the following morning to take me to Billingsgate Fish Market and the first task. I am used to getting up early, but 3.00 a.m. is downright antisocial!

When I arrived at Billingsgate, the candidates were all there, kitted out in appropriate footwear and overalls. I followed my team around, duly making copious notes of everything that was said, who negotiated well and who held back, who showed common sense, and who was out of their depth. Did they buy the first piece of fish, or did they hunt around for better prices?

The task involved the candidates negotiating the purchase of fish, then going into pre-designated kitchens on-site, where they gutted and cooked their fish, before boxing it up in time to sell to the lunchtime crowd at prearranged locations (with the appropriate licences, of course!).

I have to say that after the negative impressions formed the previous evening, seeing them in action was a different story – they were focused, determined and extremely energetic. As soon as the purchases had been made, both teams were ushered into the kitchens, where the team I was following organised themselves into those who would be preparing the fish, those who would be ordering the salad and other ancillary items, and those who would be doing the cooking. Of course, I needed to be privy to every decision in order to report everything back to Alan. Once again, I noted that Karren had done the same.

Whilst all this was going on, the production director was keen to capture my first impressions. He asked me to comment on which candidates I felt were leading, which were floundering, and, more importantly, what business insights I could offer into how the task was being managed.

Well, actually, I didn't have much of a clue! I had been focusing so much on recording who had said what that I had not been considering the additional and important dimension of whether the retail pricing or margins were in line with good business practice – the very thing that I prided myself on, and which would ultimately be key to winning or losing the task!

I decided that I needed to pay attention to that going forward, and immediately noted that Richard Woods appeared to be very much in charge of things: he was controlling the flow of food from the gutting and prep areas and doing all the frying of the fish. He knew his way around the kitchen and was good at organising people. By contrast, Sam Curry was struggling with working out the quantity of ingredients, and generally with numbers, while Mergim Butaja was at a complete loss. Selina Waterman–Smith, Charleine Wain, Gary Poulton and Natalie Dean were gutting fish, and – great credit to them – they didn't stop for five hours straight.

The team was on a tight schedule and, just after 11.00 a.m., they split up, with one group going to Camden Market and the other to King's Cross Station. Now the skill set had changed from negotiating and buying, manufacturing and pricing, to pure selling. Richard certainly had a way with customers, while Charleine stood out as an unbelievably good salesperson, relentless in her determination to sell fish to anyone who came anywhere near her.

Once the lunchtime trade had settled down, the team moved from Camden Market and decided to take the balance of their produce to local shops. As it approached 5.00 p.m., they joined the other members of their team at King's Cross to sell whatever they had left to commuters on their way home, reducing their prices in an attempt to sell out.

Of course, throughout the day, I had been emailing Alan to give him progress reports and information on who was leading, who was selling, and who was not up to the mark. This was punctuated by regular demands from the production director to provide my 'extraordinary' business insights into what was going on. Put on the spot, I felt that everything I offered sounded trite or too obvious – and whenever I did have something 'earth-shattering' to impart, my ability to state it succinctly on camera was lacking.

I got home late that evening, and was very tired indeed. I had been up since well before the crack of dawn, on my feet all day, rushing all over the place, writing notes, observing and emailing Alan – quite different from my relatively sedentary lifestyle. The warnings from Alan and Karren about the stamina required, which I had so carelessly dismissed, were now sinking in. Never mind the candidates – how was *I* going to get to the end of this process?!

Despite my aching muscles, however, I had a true feeling of exhilaration. It had been a terrific experience. I went away with two main impressions, which have stayed with me during every single task I have since been involved in over my two seasons as 'Lord Sugar's advisor'.

The first is how incredible all the candidates are. How hard they work, how resourceful they are, and how much they want to win *The Apprentice* to get the investment and change their lives. I truly admire them all. Just reflect on what they have to put themselves through: having a camera in your face all day, every day, recording for possible broadcast everything you say and do; having to be able to be function effectively as a team player and as a leader; grasping quickly what each task involves and how best to utilise the time and resources in order to prevail; having Karren or me observing your every utterance; and ultimately being brought into the boardroom to submit to harsh analysis in intimidating surroundings. All of this while living with strangers who, at one moment can appear to be your friends, and the next could throw you under the bus in an effort to save themselves from the ignominy of being fired! And through all that, not having contact with family or access to the things we take for granted, like newspapers, television, internet and normal daily interaction. Be under no illusion, this experience is not a walk in the park, and the candidates are, for the most part, quite extraordinary.

My second impression is of how exceptional the production team are. I cannot begin to express what a pleasure and delight it is to work with them. They are professional in every sense of the word. The crew, as I believe the cameramen, Sound and Lighting are known, are incredible. If Karren and I have to be at a venue at 6.00 a.m., that means that the crew have been there setting everything up some two hours earlier. When I leave at the end of the day, they are still at it. And to top it all, they are such fun to work with. Their patience knows no bounds. I have never seen any of them ever show frustration, and, working with a rank amateur like me, they jolly me along when I lose my train of thought mid-sentence, or have to repeat myself because passing traffic has drowned out my voice. On more than one occasion, we have all burst out laughing after I have said something outrageous, or been unable to engage my brain, and, after numerous attempts, am still incapable of stringing a sentence together.

The day after the completion of every task, the candidates are summoned to the boardroom, and, at the end of that day, as Alan points out each time, 'at least one of you will be fired'. However, before that drama unfolds, Alan, Karren and I assemble in Alan's studio office.

Although Alan has received, collated and read through all the emails sent through by Karren and me during the tasks, he always wants these reams of notes to be condensed onto one side of an A4! Karren gets one half and I get the other.

I usually take my seat on a chair next to the sofa allotted to Karren. I only mention this because, from my vantage point, I can see Karren's notebook in which she has written all her original notes. These are incredibly neatly written on the right-hand side of the notepad, with bullet points clearly marked on the left. In all my working life, I have never seen anything so well organised. But that's not the full story. Karren has gathered her thoughts and knows exactly what information is important for Alan to know, and is able to articulate and extract the key events. Her oral summary of the task is also a work of precise art: her points are jotted down by Alan on the left-hand side of a sheet of A4 and her concluding remark coincides with the last available line on this piece of paper.

It is probably best not to go into any detail about *my* notebook. Suffice to say, it is unintelligible to the untrained eye. I go through the same process and attempt to pick out the salient points.

With that element of the procedure complete, Alan tells us to feel free to interject if the candidates make assertions in the boardroom that are incorrect, or if there are specific points that need to be brought out into the open. Again, Karren knows exactly the tone to adopt and interjects with 'Tell Lord Sugar what really happened . . . ' This comment usually leads to a fruitful area of discussion or, more likely, discord, and eventually the truth emerges. She plays her role to perfection.

Having just completed series twelve at the time of writing this chapter, I have to say that Karren is fun to work with. She is disarmingly honest, and great company when we spend time together on tasks. There is no competitive element to the roles we play – we are there to complement each other and, above all, provide all the support and the 'eyes and ears' that Alan needs. Notwithstanding that, some friendly rivalry has emerged. At heart, we are really serious about doing our best to ensure that the information provided to Alan gives him the best insight into his decision about who he fires and ultimately who he hires. But we have moments of banter, too.

As I have said, Karren's notes are impressive, but mine have certainly improved now that I have got the hang of it. Indeed, on one occasion, Karren must have been a bit below par, because I was convinced that my numerous and prolific emails to Alan were more comprehensive and authoritative than hers, and I told her so. So, when we got to Alan's studio office to give him the A4 summary, I had a good feeling. Of course, Karren is sharp, and before Alan could start writing, she smiled at him and said, 'Alan, I've kept my emails to you very concise, because I know you don't like to be over-burdened by lengthy emails.' Alan replied that he had noted that and was 'very pleased'. Karren winked at me. She's a class act, and I am sure Alan smiled knowingly.

For my part, in all the years I have been involved, advising Alan has been my sole aim and preoccupation. As an advisor, there are challenges along the way to ensure that, as they progress towards the 'final five', who will submit themselves to the pressure of the interviews, the candidates have opportunities to demonstrate their range of abilities. For instance, very often, one candidate might dominate a task and lead the others into a high-risk strategy. Even if that strategy leads to a win for the team, and that candidate comes away feeling empowered, his or her penchant for risk is noted.

One of the more difficult aspects of the advisor's role is to keep quiet and try not to show any sign of emotion during the tasks. It would be wrong to give out hints to the candidates, and would somewhat invalidate the point of the exercise. That is not to say, in any case, that I always have the right answer to the problem. On more than one occasion I would have made different choices, but the path taken by the candidates still proved successful.

Then again, sometimes the clues seem to be obvious to everyone but the candidates. During the pop-up shop task in Manchester in series eleven, the team I was observing had purchased a range of goods from a large, local cash-and-carry wholesaler. The object of the exercise was to entice customers into the shop with some very keenly priced goods and then sell them other products at full mark-up and healthy margins.

Although Gary Poulton was a highly experienced retailer and the project manager on the task, the pricing strategy was poorly executed and even the so-called loss leaders, such as toothpaste, received the full mark-up, priced at £2. Well, that was not good, but, worse still, none of the team had considered checking out the competition. Just two shops along the mall was a pound shop, and we all know what price they sell at! I was so tempted to tell them to have a walk around the shopping centre, but that would have been unfair on the other team and made a mockery of the task and my role in the process.

Invariably there are moments of drama and unexpected things happen. That is the nature of the process and no different from what happens in the world of business. People sometimes get promoted to positions above their level of ability. Sometimes, the growth or complexity of a company outweighs an individual's ability to keep up or change. An outstanding salesman does not necessarily make a good general manager.

During series eleven, one of the candidates, Scott Saunders, who had done well in earlier tasks, had gone through a rough couple of weeks and been criticised in the boardroom. Alan had 'marked his card' and said that he was very lucky still to be in the process. At the end of the board-room session, during which his team actually won the task, Scott remained rooted to his seat. Alan looked at him quiz-zically and Scott just said that he wanted to leave the process. I was momentarily stunned, but Scott had hit a brick wall and could not go on. I suppose one has to give him credit for recognising that he was not up to the challenge.

*

Although viewing figures for *The Apprentice* remain very high, and all the candidates who have won the £250,000 investment have gone on to develop profitable businesses and create employment opportunities, there are those who question the relevance of the tasks and the programme to the world of business.

I would strongly take issue with the critics on those points. I firmly believe that the challenges candidates encounter on *The Apprentice* mirror those faced by businesses and individuals in the workplace. Buying, selling, sourcing, negotiating, costing, presenting to experts, pitching, listening, quickly assimilating information, and managing and dealing with strong characters are all relevant. As are coping with situations that are outside one's comfort zone, managing success and failure, working within time constraints, leading a team, being part of a team, making decisions, operating within a limited budget, preparing a CV and business plan, and having them scrutinised and analysed. Being challenged in the boardroom and understanding when to keep quiet and when to speak up. Composing your thoughts and ideas and framing them to persuade others. The list goes on and on.

And bear in mind that the candidates do all that with a camera in their face, with either Karren or me observing their every action, and, to top it all, facing Lord Sugar. Frankly, if you can survive that, you can achieve almost anything!

Indeed, to my mind, in its current format, *The Apprentice*

is even more relevant and instructive in today's increasingly uncertain times, as the economy shifts from one in which young people can expect to be employed to one where the focus is on starting their own businesses. Social media and technology have played a big part in this shift and no doubt will continue to do so.

I feel like I have benefited from my change of role – I relish watching the candidates develop under such intense pressure and scrutiny, the new situations and people I encounter, and the fun of being on set with such a professional group of people. It's exhilarating – and totally exhausting. Being on telly isn't for the faint-hearted!

The wheel turns full circle

In May 2009, I received a call out of the blue from the vice chancellor's office at the University of West London, where some twenty years earlier I had studied for an MBA. Professor Peter John was inviting me to have a private lunch with him. I thought to myself, What could that all be about? I accepted the invitation, and immediately googled him to try and find out what all those letters after his name related to.

As I entered the main door of the university and walked along the long corridors with lecture rooms on either side, I had mixed emotions. The place had barely changed from the very first time I went there as a nineteen-year-old undergraduate. I also recalled the enjoyment and knowledge I had gained there when doing my MBA. As students filed past me, chatting away, I couldn't help but notice how young they looked, and that made me feel very old!

When I was a student, I occasionally had lunch at Pillars, the award-winning on-campus restaurant, where the catering and hospitality students prepared and served lunches at subsidised prices. This was where I met Peter for lunch. He was accompanied by Luna Sidhu, who was introduced to me as the director of Development and Alumni Relations.

I had imagined that Peter would be a stuffy academic, but that could not have been further from the truth. He was very affable and engaging, talking about his love of sport (particularly Welsh rugby) and wanting to know about my time at Spurs. Luna was softly spoken and incredibly pleasant and friendly. The lunch was beautifully cooked and served, and Peter mentioned that I had been something of a star student on the MBA course. At that point, it was obvious to me that they had made some administrative error and were speaking to the wrong guy! I was told that my course tutor at the time, Mike Cumming, had even noted on my file that I was 'one to watch'. Peter went on to say that he and Luna had been tracking my career progression and successes and, as a result, wanted to offer me an honorary doctorate. I rapidly went through the emotional gears: from absolutely dumbfounded to overjoyed. I accepted the honour. Finally, I had been awarded a *tableau d'honneur*!

Peter also invited me to join one of the university committees. I confess the idea didn't really appeal to me that much but, how could I refuse? The chairman of the committee was Chris Humphries, the chair of the board of governors, and he ran the meetings expertly. Notwithstanding that, after just three meetings I quit. I felt that if I stayed on, I would inevitably say something untoward. In my opinion, the topics under review were not ones I felt I could contribute to. As it turned out, I probably was not alone in thinking that, because shortly after my departure, that committee folded.

In 2012, Luna contacted me again and asked if I could meet with her on a matter of some importance. The university was about to embark on an exciting redevelopment of the main campus on St Mary's Road, Ealing. The estimated cost was in the region of £50 million. Luna showed me artists' impressions of what the new building would look like. The clever use of space and design features were impressive – I remember that a new library, superb facilities for the performing arts, social and technology hubs and new lecture theatres were all thoughtfully and creatively accommodated. If the project could come to fruition, it would be transformational to the whole look of the campus. Very exciting, but what did that have to do with me?

Luna explained that the vice chancellor had been very astute and rationalised a number of the outlying campuses, so, for the first time in many years, the university had some of the funding in place to invest in this redevelopment programme. A high-level committee was being assembled to oversee the project and fundraise for it. Sir Rocco Forte – the hugely successful hotelier – was mentioned amongst other luminaries who had been invited to join the committee, which also included the chancellor, Laurence Geller, Peter John and a number of members of the board of governors, along with Luna's department acting as the conduit. The vice chancellor believed that I was the best person to chair the committee.

My immediate reaction was that if so many high profile and successful entrepreneurs were joining the committee, then let one of *them* be the chair. Luna, in her quiet, but persistent, way, assured me that I would be the best person to keep the other members 'in check'. I tentatively agreed to undertake the role, with the proviso that if it was anything like the previous university committee, I would not be hanging around.

There was some tension amongst the committee members at the first meeting. A number of them must have been *Apprentice* fans and were somewhat apprehensive. Alistair Telfer, the chair of the Alumni Board and a larger-than-life character, ventured to let me know after the meeting that I was not at all like my television persona. I detected a twinge of disappointment in his tone.

As it turned out, it worked out really well. I chaired the committee for over three years, and during that time the redevelopment was completed. The campus at St Mary's Road looks spectacular and every bit as impressive as the artists' impressions. Apart from the joy of seeing the transformation, the committee members were all absolutely wonderful people to be associated with.

The whole redevelopment project was really enjoyable. People have a real passion for this university and it was heartening to see them dedicate so much time to raising money and seeing the project through. Luna and her colleagues Maja and Natalie worked tirelessly throughout, and, although I was the front man, they were the ones who really kept all the initiatives going. With David Foskett, the head of the school of hospitality at the university, they even organised a highly successful gala fundraising event at the Dorchester Hotel on 17 January 2014.

After the January 2014 campaign committee meeting,

Peter drew me to one side and said, 'Claude, we want to raise the profile and relaunch the business school. One of the initiatives is to offer naming rights to the school.' I naturally assumed that they wanted Lord Sugar to be involved, but as it turned out, they wanted me to lend my name to it! I told Peter that I wasn't a big name, and they would be better advised to look elsewhere. But Peter was adamant: they wanted me. I was an alumnus of the university and, most importantly, successful in business. This was the key factor, and not, for example, that they expected a donation from me. I felt deeply honoured once I'd established that they simply wanted my name and some involvement in promoting the business school. I was chuffed, and thought about the irony of life that had brought me to this position.

All smiles at the launch of the Claude Littner Business School.

On 8 October 2014, Alan Sugar was kind enough to launch the Claude Littner Business School at the University of West London. He said, 'Claude's involvement in the business school that now bears his name will provide the impetus for students to benefit from academic study, coupled with a strong practical and commercial focus, enabling them to get ahead in the job market. Those who work hard and exhibit strong business acumen have the best chance of becoming future business leaders.'

*

Since then, my professional focus has been very much on the university. I have rationalised my thinking and decided that I don't want to be involved in running, or turning around, businesses any more. I have neither the required stamina nor the will. Every now and then, I am approached by banks and venture capitalists, but I always say 'no'. I have left that world behind. It's much more satisfying to try to put something back into the education system in whatever way I can.

At the university, I think of myself as a minister without portfolio. I am very keen to lend my support where I believe I can add value. This can be making contacts with large local businesses, promoting new ways of doing things, raising the profile of the business school through whatever celebrity status I have achieved, dropping into seminars and providing encouragement, or speaking to prospective students and their parents at open days.

I have three basic aims.

The first is to do what I can to foster good relations within the business community, encouraging companies to provide work experience for our students, or engaging with the university to provide/facilitate short courses or part-time/executive courses for some of their managers.

The second is to encourage students to make the most of their time at the business school. Many are first-generation university students, and some come from disadvantaged backgrounds. They need the confidence and encouragement to see the course through.

My third aim is to make every effort to ensure that the course of study combines the formal academic elements with a very practical understanding of the world of work. To that end, the business school invites entrepreneurs and corporate executives to talk to the students and answer questions. This is supplemented by case studies, which provide further insight into how companies face real competitive challenges.

From my own experience, I learned that I really only came into my own when I made the connection between study and 'real life', and I think that's the same for quite a lot of people. If we, at the university, can offer up an environment that makes the links between the classroom and the outside world stronger and clearer, then I think we'll be helping those who have real ability, but do not necessarily excel in their studies.

Fortunately for the students, I don't teach the academic courses. Instead, I focus on making contacts with local businesses, as I think this is the lifeblood of the business school. The idea is to bridge the gap between what has been taught at university, which is necessarily academic and theoretical, and the students' understanding of the very fast-paced, dynamic business environment – where new ideas are failing and succeeding all the time.

If you haven't got that contact with the outside world,

you're just ploughing through the same old theories and practices, which means you're in danger of not giving the students the best insight and preparation into how business works. Giving students that exposure is imperative in ensuring they have the best possible chance of success.

This connection with real business is also great for the academics – no matter how brilliant they are – because they need to be at the forefront of what's going on. It's incredibly important that they have the opportunity to visit companies to hear about the latest thinking and most recent trends, then bring that message back to the students through case studies and from the research they have conducted. It shows students different ways to problem-solve, and, if I had to sum up the world of business, to me it's all about problem-solving.

The university has a great network of business contacts through its other schools on campus. For example, the hospitality school within the university has excellent contacts with British Airways and all the hotels in the area. The business school is already tapping into that contacts list and the high-level opportunities it provides. What I'm trying to do is extend the network further into areas where perhaps we haven't got as good an address book as we should.

I've been lucky to go into some of these places and have a conversation with the chief executive, or the HR director, to see if we can have a two-way, reciprocal arrangement, whereby the company sends us some of their managers for short courses or MBAs, and some of our students can enter into work experience placements that sometimes lead to permanent roles.

I think I've been quite successful in setting up those kinds of arrangements, and perhaps having some kind of public profile helps me in that – although it's difficult to say that conclusively, since a lot of companies are very grateful to have a connection with the university, anyway.

There is a social responsibility angle to this, too. We have a lot of students who are the first generation in their family to attend university. They have made huge sacrifices to get there, instead of going straight into whatever work they could find, which their families might have put them under huge pressure to do. I think it is incumbent on us to do the very best we can for them.

One exciting innovation at the business school is that some of the courses will focus on start-ups. In my day, you got your qualification, chose an industry and went after a job; now, we're focusing on trying to make the courses very relevant to those individuals who feel they have a good business idea that they'd like to turn into a viable proposition.

The university is responding to those students in two ways. The first is to make sure the courses prepare the students for what a start-up will actually involve. It tackles the issues you might face in just setting up a company and the problems you will encounter starting out on your own. To offer first-hand experience, we bring in mentors – people who run their own businesses – to talk about the challenges, opportunities and benefits.

Secondly, when a student graduates, we intend to give them the opportunity to test out their idea or take it one stage further by giving them a period of incubation in the university. This will entail having a dedicated hub on campus, shared with others who are similarly engaged, and the university will provide free facilities, such as telephones, internet access, premises, mentoring, and whatever other assistance is required for the fledgling company to get off the ground, and move from its first stage of business idea to something more tangible. The point is that hopefully some of those early blunders that entrepreneurs make can be challenged and avoided. There will also be the opportunity, when this initiative is properly up and running, to invite some entrepreneurs or angel investors to come along and look at some of the ideas, and maybe invest in them, too.

In the end, this is about bridging the gap between academia and real life. Where this university *is* particularly strong is that a lot of the courses are not purely academic – they are very practical and career-orientated, with an underlying ethos of bringing the theoretical and the practical together. Long term, we want to encourage people with great ideas who want to start their own companies.

This new approach is partly in reaction, too, to the fact that universities are businesses now. They have to provide a good 'product' because they have to justify the fees they charge – just like anyone else. The university has to provide a quality service and academics now also have to ensure that they are providing 'value for money'. This is a fundamental shift in the relationship between teachers and students, and one that I'm trying to help with, because academics aren't always the most natural business people!

Bearing this in mind, it was interesting that at the launch of the business school, I met the principal of the University of Cyprus, which is a bit like an affiliate of the University of West London: they run business courses in conjunction with us. It was the first time I'd realised that we had 'offshoots' in other parts of the world. It dawned on me that this could be a very important part of the growth and development of the university. Over the years, there had been increasing abuse of the system by bogus students coming to study at non-existent universities, and so on. We've all seen the reports in the newspapers and I think the government were right to clamp down on that. It does, however, make it quite difficult for overseas students to come here legitimately to study. So, the opportunity to have 'satellite' universities in different countries, where students can attend and get a University of West London degree, was one that we, and a number of other UK universities, latched on to.

In June 2015, I took a call from a charity asking me to come along as a guest speaker and give out awards. It turned out to be a very pleasant evening indeed, and the organisers and charity committee could not have been friendlier to Thelma and me. All those receiving awards, as well as all the other participants, were extremely dedicated, giving up a part of their lives to doing something for the benefit of others.

During the course of that evening, I was introduced to a host of interesting people. Two, however, stood out. One of them was the chief executive of Bank Leumi, Eli Katzav. And the other was introduced to me with the remark 'You two have got something in common.' It transpired that this person, Nissim Levy, had, together with a partner, set up a private university in Marbella, Spain, called the Marbella International University Centre (MIUC). In fact, Nissim was the event sponsor that evening. We got talking and his project sounded really interesting. By pure coincidence, I was going to Marbella on holiday the following week, so I asked whether I could visit the university while I was there.

During my visit, Nissim, a doctor of chemistry and a

former NASA researcher who gave up his academic career to become a highly successful entrepreneur, couldn't have been more accommodating – and I also met his business partner, Predrag Jevremovic, an unbelievably warm-hearted man who has had a very varied and successful career, is bursting with new ideas and has established himself in Marbella with numerous lucrative business interests. The university itself was a joy to behold, with a location that brought a smile to my face: an elevated position with sea views, overlooking Marbella, and just a short walk from the beach and port. The university building itself was purpose-built and developed with great thought. The lecture rooms and overall facilities were state of the art, and the academic and support staff were of the highest calibre, and extremely friendly.

MIUC attracts students from all over the world and all the courses are taught in English. Nissim and Predrag intend this to be a commercial venture. However, the underlying commercial aspect belies their passion for this university to be a real seat of learning and academic excellence. I wish them every success: they are two of the most genuine, engaging, generous and fun-loving people I have met.

While I was looking around, it occurred to me that this might be a wonderful location for students to obtain fully accredited Claude Littner Business School degrees, validated and awarded by the University of West London. I discussed this with Nissim and Predrag, and they immediately latched on to the idea. Indeed, they were already running accredited business degrees from the Singidunum University of Belgrade in Serbia under the Bologna Process education model, designed to ensure comparability in the standards and quality of higher education qualifications. They were very enthusiastic, however, about the prospect of being able to award British (and London at that!) university degrees, and very keen to see if they could forge a link with the University of West London.

I returned to the UK and discussed the idea with the vice chancellor, who was very interested in developing a network of satellite university institutions, and, indeed, had already set up a number in the Far East. MIUC would be able to offer students the opportunity of obtaining a UK degree with all its advantages – particularly to those who might struggle to obtain a student visa. For the University of West London, the benefits were an extension of its brand and know-how into mainland Europe, as well as a new revenue stream. From a commercial and structural viewpoint, this was a win–win.

With the utmost goodwill, both academic institutions embarked on a lengthy process of assessment. At MIUC, Mirjana Stefanovic led the team who provided the huge amount of information required to ensure that MIUC satisfied the stringent quality assurance required to award University of West London business degrees to their students. After a year of exchange of information and meetings, MIUC met the criteria and received a positive audit. From the academic year 2016–17 students will have the opportunity of applying to embark on a course of study in Marbella that will culminate in an honours degree validated by the Claude Littner Business School at the University of West London and Marbella International University Centre.

As a follow-on from the partnership with MIUC, the vice chancellor and deputy vice chancellor, Anthony Woodman, who has been very helpful to me at the business school, will be visiting and possibly engaging with the University of Belgrade – and its 17,000 students. The potential for extending the reach of the university further into Europe looks very encouraging, particularly in light of Brexit, because we have established partnerships with European universities offering our courses. I'm excited to see what the future brings.

*

Whenever I chat to students, my strong advice is: enjoy your university years and soak up as much knowledge as you can. You never know what piece of information or skill will be useful in the future, and, even if it doesn't prove useful, knowledge brings its own rewards. Look outwards; don't look down. You may not know exactly what you are looking for yet – but you can still look out to see what is actually happening around you. Ask yourself: How can I get involved in that? How can I slot in? How can I do it better? Always think about the opportunities on offer, how you can create value or what you can bring to your role.

For my part, I resolved to add value to the university. In March 2015, I submitted my CV to the dean of the business school, the vice chancellor and the board of governors, coupled with my achievements and plans to further promote and enhance the research community and external profile of the business school. I was made a visiting professor.

The university has become an important part of my life and I plan to use my profile and entrepreneurial skills as best I can to help it develop further. I am excited by the

From left to right: Chris Humphries, chair of the board of governors, Professor Peter John, vice chancellor, visiting professor Claude Littner, Lord Farringdon, pro-chancellor, and Laurence Geller, chancellor.

challenges that UWL affords me and delighted by the fact that everyone there seems genuinely pleased with my involvement and the interest I show in everything. Last week, in between meetings, I decided to pop into one of the classes to watch and listen. I liked it. It was very interesting and I think the students got a kick out of me being there. I didn't contribute much – that was not the purpose – but I did answer some questions and perhaps it gave the class and school a bit more enthusiasm and energy. Maybe I can inspire them, because *I* am inspired.

I think I have come full circle: back to school again, only this time I am most definitely 'front of the class'!

Amounting to something

The shape of my business life at the time of writing is a lot less complex than at any other stage. Since 2009, in addition to my activities at the university, I have been chairman of Alan Sugar's companies. This came about after Alan was ennobled by Gordon Brown and took his seat on the Labour benches in the House of Lords. As we were in the run-up to a general election, the party in opposition (the Conservatives) had claimed a conflict of interest, given Alan's role as the government's enterprise tsar. They wanted him either to give up his role in *The Apprentice* or to relinquish all the directorships of his companies. I never understood what the fuss about, but Alan asked me to step in, become a director and chair his companies. I happily did so, and have remained in situ ever since.

There's no need to dwell on all those different business interests here, save to say that I enjoy being involved. For me, every board meeting and every business discussion provides a new and exciting insight into Alan's and his children's approach to business, problem-solving and value-creating.

Alan's sons Simon and Daniel have inherited his business acumen and embrace his business principles. Each of them runs a division of the private office and displays expertise and professionalism of the highest order. Technological advances, the medical and scientific research and innovation brought about by generations of gifted individuals, new corporate know-how, the legal system and government intervention have all transformed every part of our everyday lives, but, for me, the core values of integrity, respect and decency in the way we conduct ourselves and behave towards others are the cornerstones of working life. Alan's sons display those values in all their business dealings.

As part of my remit, I also became chairman of Viglen, where I was very pleased to join forces with its chief executive, Bordan Tkachuk, previously of *The Apprentice*, and Mike Ray, the finance director who was so very helpful to me back in my earliest days at Amstrad France. Viglen had gone from selling computer equipment to selling solutions and growing the academies and schools part of the business. Alan's objective was to further develop the company with a view to then selling it. In 2014, that objective was realised.

Simon Sugar runs Amscreen and we work well together. Amscreen is now Europe's leading digital signage solutions company with a strategic alliance with Clear Channel. It is, quite naturally, the technology innovator and has set up a purpose-built factory from scratch in Bolton, where its giant, state-of-the-art digital signage screens are assembled. I have no doubt that this business will be hugely successful, and I am thrilled to be involved in the action, albeit in a non-executive role.

For some time, I have also been advising start-ups and early stage companies, and will from now on actively take a greater interest by way of funding and taking strategic stakes in some of the companies. I think this will continue to provide me with an opportunity of helping growth companies and maintaining my involvement in business.

*

One of the most amazing and disturbing things about life is just how fast it slips by, and how quickly one moves from one stage onto another, and then another. It is therefore so very important to enjoy each stage and make the most of it. Before you know it, it has passed.

When I look back on my life, I can say that I have had a whale of a time. My glass is not half full – it is overflowing! All the obstacles I have encountered pale into insignificance when set alongside the joy of being alive, of being lucky enough to have lived in a peace-loving country largely protected from the chaos the world finds itself in, and, of course, of being surrounded by a loving family and friends.

Being involved in *The Apprentice* is a small case in point about the importance of enjoying yourself. Last year, Thelma and I were invited to the National Television Awards. Alan said that going was a waste of time because the programme was not going to win anything. For me, that was not the point – I was thrilled to be invited and to have the experience.

I squeezed Thelma's hand as we walked down the red carpet – pure fantasy, as the banks of photographers excitedly snapped away and called for us to glance in their direction. Meanwhile, fans gathered in something approaching a frenzy as we walked past and made our way into the reception area. Once we were in the O2 Centre, I was sure I must be imagining things, because I thought I heard my name being shouted out by lots of people in the audience. I looked around, and, sure enough, fans were beckoning for me to come over to them for selfies.

As Alan had predicted, although nominated, *The Apprentice* lost out to *The Great British Bake Off.* Following the show was an after party – never been to one of those either! As I am not a fan of soaps or reality TV, I did not realise that the people approaching me to tell me how amazing I was and to request selfies, were actually the stars of those programmes. It was absolutely surreal . . . and a lot of fun. I wouldn't have missed it for the world.

Of course, such attention is not as much fun when you're doing a piece to camera at 7.00 p.m., three weeks into the punishing filming schedule, and fans, in their unbridled enthusiasm, shout your name or decide to get in front of the camera, but I guess one has to take the rough with the smooth!

At times like those, I realise that I have come a long way from my frustrating and disappointing school days, and I reflect that there are many examples of those who left school early because they had either failed to get the grades, were not academic, or just wanted to get out and earn a living. I respect those choices, but my situation differs somewhat. While I was never a good student, and had difficulty passing exams, I remained undeterred and was prepared to sit – and *resit* – tests in order to achieve the grades required, thereby enabling me to reach my objective. I have always been absolutely, doggedly single-minded.

My purpose in writing this book is to show that you don't need to be an A-grade student to succeed (although that certainly helps!). As you have read, my progression was not without hitches and numerous mistakes along the way. I really want to encourage young people to have faith in their abilities, to be confident in their approach to work and to try different things until they find their niche.

Of course, so many young people face far greater challenges early in their lives than an indifferent performance at school and a 'hernia'. Difficulties come from so many different areas now: personal, financial, family, social, language, integration and discrimination – but notwithstanding these barriers, what you need to do is to find something you are good at and, better still, enjoy, then see if you can make inroads into that field. From my experience, companies tend to promote from within if appropriate.

The key to it all is to do the best you can. That's all you can ask of yourself, or that anyone can ask of you. However, your best is always changing, as you develop more skills, as you study and learn from others, as you engage your brain and perhaps discover a host of additional things you are capable of, which you hadn't appreciated earlier.

When you take your first steps in your working life, everything can look baffling, complex and maybe incomprehensible but, I think, if you prepare yourself during your studies by getting as much insight into yourself and how companies operate, then, when you start out, it will make for a smoother, less stressful experience. In business, it is important to take time to understand the culture and see how people interact. Being alert, working things out and demonstrating a willingness to learn, getting involved and being a good team member – these are all important traits.

There is a temptation at the start to pretend you know stuff, but you probably don't, so it is always worth asking questions, at the right time, in the right way and to the right person, in order to get a better appreciation of how things work and what is expected of you. I've recounted how I nearly always did this when getting stuck into something new by seeking out the good, knowledgeable people at the company.

Increasingly, graduates and school leavers are finding that gaining employment is becoming much harder and, in certain instances, very much more competitive. My route into Unilever many decades ago was fortuitous, and I believe that a proactive approach to targeting companies might still be a part of the armoury of getting an interview, and potentially landing a job. Nothing is easy. On one occasion, when I was out of work, I sat at my desk every day and sent out copies of my CV and covering letter. Getting a job is a full-time job in itself! I must have sent out at least a hundred applications and I kept the file for many years, as a reminder of what I had to do in order to get back into gainful employment.

Consequently, starting your own business is a route many people are taking. Although it requires a special mindset to run your own business, it can be a really viable alternative to being employed by someone else. The technology that is available today absolutely enables people to get going much more easily than before, to make a start without much capital, and to announce yourself to the global marketplace.

There are many more examples of new routes to starting out, such as the rise of crowdfunding platforms, angel investors and companies that offer unsecured loans to businesses that do not yet have track records. Although traditional routes to employment might be more difficult to follow today, there is now a broader range of opportunity for anyone with a good idea, ability and a burning desire to succeed and make their dreams come true.

The Apprentice is just a small embodiment of this – each year, one person who shows courage, determination and business acumen in working through the tasks, will get the £250,000 investment and the chance to change their life.

My role and profile in *The Apprentice* have more to do with the requirements of reality TV than my true attitude to the candidates, whom I admire wholeheartedly. I hope that this is borne out by the chapters on the programme in this book. Anyone who is willing and able to put themselves through such a rigorous process deserves a huge amount of credit.

*

While my *Apprentice* character has evolved into what others have called the 'hard man' of the show, my involvement with the business school, and the way I have recounted my career in this book, shows another, more comprehensive, side of my character. I want to help young people get on and do the best they can. I hope I've demonstrated that hard work, focus and determination, coupled with business acumen and a common-sense approach to solving problems, were actually what drove me to make something of myself – and that my example might give young people the confidence to go out and do the best they can. If that's in management, as an entrepreneur or stacking shelves, it doesn't matter – the key is to do it well, and be happy with what you do and achieve.

These days my determination is still as strong as ever, but I'm not as aggressive in my pursuit of the objectives I set myself. I've mellowed and matured – a little! I've learned to become more relaxed and take things in my stride. As a consequence, I feel more at ease with myself now than I ever have done in the past.

When I look at myself in the mirror, I sometimes catch a glimpse of my father and mother in some of my features. Not that I need a reminder – I carry them with me all the time. They were remarkable people and wonderful parents. I try to emulate their solid family values and lifestyle, and pass these principles on to my children and grandchildren. I have been unbelievably fortunate in having a wonderful wife, children, family and friends.

Throughout my career, I have endeavoured to separate the personal and the professional, and have taken care to avoid possible conflicts of interest or putting myself in a situation where relationships can hamper good business judgement. Whether as chairman or chief executive, I have always felt it unwise to get too 'pally' with other members of the board or senior staff, because when you have to make tough decisions for the good of the business, you can't afford any sense that you are either granting favours or exacting revenge; I would never want to be seen as anything other than completely impartial. So, I've steered a course of independence and remained aloof.

Once I have left a company, I feel more inclined to relax and be sociable and friendly with those who I might have been 'offish' with before. For example, at Tottenham, where I have retained my former director privileges, I still go to most home matches. Everyone is so very friendly (probably relieved that I am not there to terrorise them!), and I enjoy chatting and having a laugh with ex-players, club legends, former directors and staff.

It is the same with the candidates on *The Apprentice*. I never give them any encouragement during the process and, indeed, as you will have noticed in the interviews, I can be brutal if their CVs or business plans fall short. However, when the show ends, I am keen to talk to them and, if asked, offer advice as to how they might progress or reposition their business idea.

*

The world is a very different place now to when I was growing up. It feels harsher, less caring and more competitive. I think it's good to have goals, to aspire to certain things and, for me, it was always to do the very best at whatever job or opportunity I am given. When I am asked for advice I say that goals are important, but the goals and their pursuit have to make you happy. Balance is important, but I think if you achieve what you set out to achieve, then other things (such as money or success) will follow – and the feeling of achievement is worth it in itself.

It has always been important for me to challenge myself, and I have a competitive streak that is in my DNA. For example, when skiing, you can choose the easier green or blue runs, or opt for the more difficult red one. They are not for me. I take the hazardous black run. And when I get to the foot of the piste, and look back up at the mountain I have just negotiated, I feel great that I made it – a real sense of achievement (and relief). That's how I have approached life. I am not a risk-taker, not a thrill-seeker, but I've always felt the need to push myself, to get to the place where I'm satisfied that I've proved myself. And overall, in my own way, I think I have – but I've had to be single-minded.

Acknowledgements

During the course of writing this book about my life in business, I have brought back to mind some of the people who have had an influence on me and relived a number of company experiences that I had almost completely forgotten about.

I would like to thank David Wilson and particularly Martin Toseland for all their encouragement, interest and skill in steering me in the right direction, teasing out my thoughts about events and extracting the business lessons. I really enjoyed the time we spent together and already miss our coffee and croissant sessions.

Meri Pentikäinen, the commissioning editor at Piatkus/ Little, Brown Book Group was enthusiastic about publishing my idea for a book from our very first meeting and has been supportive and constructive throughout, and also such a lovely person to deal with.

Thanks to Alison Sturgeon, the copyeditor who enriched my words, and the lawyer, Nicola Thatcher, who toned them down! Indeed, I am very grateful to everyone at the publishers who has contributed to the finished book. I also thank Alan Sugar, Hannah Wyatt and Cal Turner for making such helpful comments on specific areas of the manuscript.

The book publishing world is new to me, and I got a glimpse of how friendly and collaborative the people at Little, Brown Book Group are when they invited me to host their quiz night. A great turnout and such a truly convivial atmosphere. Naturally, I had to admonish Charlie King, the managing director, for being disruptive, but mainly for being an Arsenal fan! I felt empowered that evening, because I had all the answers to the quiz questions. At least that would have been the case had Richard Beswick, Andrew McAleer and Nick Ross actually provided me with all the right answers!

The fact is that I would not be alive today but for the care provided by the dedicated doctors and nurses at University College Hospital. From the bottom of my heart, I want to thank my sister Tina, whose stem cells saved my life when I had cancer, and my oncologist, Professor David Linch, who achieved a miracle! My ever-loving parents and my wife were with me every single day throughout my ordeal. Thanks also to the members of my family and friends who have been close through all the good times and supported me when things seemed hopeless and I was helpless.

I have barely mentioned my sons Anthony and Alex, but I am so very proud of them both. I could not wish for more wonderful children. They are both a credit to Thelma and me, and are respected and successful in their professional and business lives. Their wives Amanda and Sarah have carried on the tradition of strong 'Littner women', and are raising their children in the best tradition and core values. We are a close family and long may that blissful harmony continue.

Last, but by no means least, I want to especially thank my wife Thelma who I have known for some forty-six years. She has always supported me in everything and given me the space and peace of mind to get on with my life in business. Thelma has been the perfect partner in every way; an outstanding person in her own right, a wonderful mother, grandmother and friend. My love and admiration for her knows no bounds.

Picture credits